"The Noahide Covenant Through the Lens of the Torah Given at Sinai"

by Rabbi Michael-Shelomo Bar-Ron
All Rights Reserved.

The fresh ruins of Noah's ark (drawn according to the theory of the late David Fasold) from the visual perspective of Moses on Mount Sinai. He is holding the *second* set of stone tablets, according to the rabbinical opinion that the second set was written in Paleo-Hebrew. The re-creation of the Paleo-Hebrew writing is original.

The drawing of the ark was inspired by and based on an original drawing by Jane Armstrong for the cover of *Noah's Ark: Adrift In Dark Waters* (June Dawes, Noahide Publishing 2000. All Rights Reserved).

GUIDE FOR THE NOAHIDE

A Complete Guide
to the Laws of the Noahide Covenant
and Key Torah Values for All Mankind

*   *   *

Rabbi Michael Shelomo Bar-Ron

Second Edition

Cover art: Design by Carol Long; Dove, iStockphoto.com, with permission

GUIDE FOR THE NOAHIDE

A Complete Guide
to the Laws of the Noahide Covenant
and Key Torah Values for All Mankind

ISBN-10: 0-9792618-7-2
ISBN-13: 978-0-9792618-7-9

Copyright © 2010 by Michael Shelomo Bar-Ron

10 9 8 7 6 5 4 3 2 1

All rights reserved. No part of this book may be used or reproduced in any manner whatsoever without written permission from the publisher, except in the case of brief quotations in reviews for inclusion in a magazine, newspaper or broadcast (including websites and webcasts).

Printed in the United States of America. For information write to Lightcatcher Books, 1204 Kissinger Ave., Springdale AR 72762, or visit our website: www.lightcatcherbooks.com

THIS BOOK CONTAINS NAMES OF GOD,
VERSES OF TORAH AND
SACRED TORAH COMMENTARY.

PLEASE TREAT IT WITH THE APPROPRIATE
SANCTITY IT DESERVES.

Rabbi Saul Zucker
Teaneck, New Jersey

3 *Iyyar* 5769, 18 days in the *'Omer*
April 27, 2009

Dear Reader,

My dear friend, Rav Michael Bar Ron, has approached me, asking for a letter of approbation for his work on the Seven Noachide Laws. I usually do not write such letters for fear that an approbation might imply agreement with every point that is contained in the book, and such agreement rarely exists. With that in mind, I have, nevertheless, agreed to write this letter, for three reasons.

First, I know Rav Michael to be a humble servant of *HaShem*, sincere, thoughtful, caring, and wise.

Second, I know that the topic of his book, sharing knowledge of the Noachide Laws to a readership that is thirsty to learn them, is of the utmost value.

Third, and perhaps most important, I know Rav Michael's *halakhic* approach – teaching Torah law in accordance with the pristine words of the *Rishonim*, the early Talmudic Sages. This approach, one that I enthusiastically endorse and embrace, reflects a genuine adherence to our authentic holy *mesorah*, the ancient and living transmission of Torah ideas and values.

As the founding *Rosh Mesivta* of the *Mesivta of North Jersey*, and as a *maggid shiur* in various venues, as well as in my capacity as Director of Day School & Educational Services of the Orthodox Union, I have seen how wisdom, knowledge, and passion can transform a student of Torah – both in the world of the yeshiva for *Bnei Yisrael*, and in the world in general for *Bnei Noach*. I wholeheartedly commend Rav Michael for his initiative, his compassion, his approach, and for his sharing the word of *HaShem* with the children of Noach throughout the world. I wish him the greatest success, and hope that this book will serve its purpose of teaching and guiding all those who sincerely seek to know their divine role within *HaShem*'s master plan for humanity.

I close with blessings of Torah for wisdom, happiness, fulfillment, and success.

Sincerely yours,

Rabbi Saul Zucker

בס"ד

Grand Rabbi Avraham Yerachmiel Rabinowits
of Ostrova-Biale
P.O.B. 41273 Jerusalem 91411 Israel, Tel. 972-2-6537593

President, American Friends
of TIFRERET DAVID - OSTROVA BIALE

הרב אברהם ירחמיאל רבינוביץ
בתה"ק מרן אדמו"ר מאסטראבא ביע"א זצללה"ה
בעל הילהבת דוד'
מאסטרובה – ביאלא
ת.ד. 41273 פעיה"ק ירושלים ת"ו 91411

נשיא
אור קדושים ירושלים ת"ו
בסייעתא דשמיא

יום ב' ג' אייר, ח"י למטמונים תשס"ט לפ"ק

מכתב ברכה והסכמה

הן בא לפני איש המעש רב הפעלים וכביר המעש לתורה ולתעודה ומיקירי אנ"ש
הע"י, הפועל מזה שנים בתחום הפצת תורה ויהדות בקרב עם ישראל קדושים באה"ק
והתפרצות ה"ה הרב מיכא-ל שלמה בר-רון שליט"א מעיר בית שמש יע"א

רו"מ המוסדות "אהל משה למען תורת משה" להפצת תורת רבינו הרמב"ם והנהגותיו

ובידו תכריך של כתבים בהם מרכז בטוטו"ד ענייני "שבע המצוות לבני נח" לחסידי
אומות העולם ויקרא שמו כי כן הוא "המדריך לבני נח", אלו היו למראה עיני
ומצאתים שהעלה בכוחו בזה ע"י עמל לבאר- העניינים על פרטיה כי רבים הם.

והנה אין עמדי אלא דברי הרמב"ם ז"ל (הל' מלכים פ"ח ה"י) שכתב בזה, וז"ל: "וכן
צוה לנו משה רבינו עפ"י הגבורה לכוף את כל באי העולם לקבל מצוות שנצטוו בני
נח" וכבר מבואר במפרשיו, דעתו, דהיינו כשהיו תחת ידינו [ובימות המשיח]. אבל
הלומדים ימצאו בהם דברים נכוחים בהיקפם לגופם של ענין.

ובאשר ידעתיו גם ידעתיו לנכון רוב עמלו ומסירות נפשו לקדש ש"ש ברבים
בפעולותיו הנשגבות לה' ולתורתו, אומר לו צלח ורכב על דבר אמת, וברכתי צרופה
שיזכה לזכות את הרבים ויפוצו מעיינותיו חוצה וחפץ ה' בידו יצליח
כעתירת הכו"ח בתפילה לקל נורא עלילה שתהא עבודתו רצויה לשמים, והמצפה לישועת ה'
ממרומים ולביאת ינון משיח צדקנו ובנין בית הבחירה בב"א

[TRANSLATION]

Grand Rabbi Avraham Yerachmiel Rabinowits
Of Ostrova-Biale
P.O.B. 41273 Jerusalem 91411 Israel, Tel: 972-2-653-7593

With the Aid of Heaven

Monday 3 Iyyar, *Hh"y le-Matmonim* 5769
[April 27, 2009]

LETTER OF BLESSING AND APPROBATION

Before me came the man of action and doer of deeds, great deeds for the sake of the Torah and Testimony, beloved of our friends and holy congregations, who has worked for years in the field of spreading Torah and Judaism among the holy People of Israel in the holy Land and abroad — **it is he, the Rabbi Michael Shelomo Bar-Ron shlit"a from the city of Beit Shemesh,** *may He send your help through holiness*, head and founder of the institutions "Ohel Moshe Lema`an Torath Moshe" — for the purpose of spreading the Torah of our master the RaMBaM and his directives.

And in his hand is a compilation of writings, which brings together — with good reasoning and wisdom — concepts of the "Seven Laws of the Descendants of Noah" for the pious of the nations of the world, and it shall be called — for so it is indeed — "The Guide for the Children of Noah" *["Guide for the Noahide"]*. My eyes have seen them, and I have found that he succeeded through hard work in clarifying the concepts to their details, for they are many. And behold, I have only the words of the RaMBaM of blessed memory (Laws of Kings ch.8, law 10) [on which to rely] who wrote about this — *may his memory be for a blessing:* **"And thus Moses commanded by the mouth of the Almighty, to bring all of those who come into the world to accept the Laws that Noah was Commanded."** And his opinion has since been clarified by his commentators [to his work], that this was for when they were under our authority (and in the days of the Messiah). However, those who study [the teachings] will find in them accurate words that cover the heart of the matter.

And being that I also know it to be true — the quantity of his work and self-sacrifice to publicly sanctify the Name of Heaven through his lofty activities for *HaShem* and His Torah — I shall tell him: *'Prosper and ride on in behalf of truth', [Psalms 45:5]* and my added blessing is that he merit to bring merit to the masses, and may his fountains [of teaching] spread outwards, and that the desire of *HaShem* [G-d] will succeed in his hand.

As a supplication *[lit. "of the author and signer"]* to G-d of Awesome Deed, that his work be desired in Heaven, and the one who anxiously awaits the Remption of *HaShem* from Above, and the coing of Yinon our righteous Messiah, and the building of the Chosen House, speedily in our days, Amen

[Signed:]

Grand Rabbi Avraham Yerachmiel Rabinovich

Son of the holy Rabbi, Master Grand Rabbi
David Matityahu of Biala
of blessed memory, author of "Lehavat David"
Of Ostrova – Biale

DEDICATIONS, THANKS, AND PRAYER

*Dedicated to HaShem, LORD Eternal,
Praised be His Name forever.*

*Dedicated to the visionary rabbis such as
the school of Ribbi Yishma`el,
who would even go into exile
to spread Torah among the nations.*

*Dedicated in living memory to
those righteous souls among the nations
Who stood by the nation of Israel
throughout the ages
Through brave self-sacrifice and
unwavering dedication,
That the light of the Torah may shine
even in the darkest of times.*

* * *

*I bow my head and prostrate fully before
the Almighty in gratitude:*

*For the sagacious guidance and editing work of my brilliant and
righteous teacher, **Mori Shelomo ben-Avraham shlit"a**,
For the support and wisdom gained from my eminent teachers
**The Grand Rebbe shlit"a of Biale-Ostrova in Jerusalem,
Aluf Abir Yehoshua Sofer – Ma`atuf Dohh `al Habbani.***

*I thank you, Master of the Universe
For the enduring patience and selfless help of my wife **Levana**
(may she be blessed with long life in health and joy),
For the patience and good behavior of **my dear children**
Gavriel Ya`aqov, Menahhem Yehudah,
Yisha`yah Meir, Avraham and El`azar.*

Master of Eternity,
In the merit of this book, may our sons be blessed and aided to grow up to keep your entire Torah zealously and correctly, finding grace in the eyes of God and man, and may the true Torah of Moshe Your servant not depart from our descendants to the end of time.

I thank you, Master of the Universe
For the advice, friendship, and encouragement of my dear friends:
The God-fearing Noahides **James D. Long,**
Andrew Overall, Jacob Scharff and **Justin Johnson**
For their support and help in editing the work,
My friend **Yehoyada` `Amos,**
and for the generous support of my noble parents,
Jacob and Ruth Barron.

They all have my heartfelt gratitude.

* * *

May my humble presentation of Your holy laws be acceptable before You HaShem, and may my words find grace in Your Eyes as a vehicle of Torah truth and clarity. I trust that You have Saved me from error, but if I have indeed erred, please Cause me to learn where and how, that I may swiftly correct the work.

May You see O HaShem our sincere pursuit of Torah truth and have compassion on Your priestly nation in these stormy, troubled times. May It be Your Will that a redeemer be raised up to be the true Messiah-king, speedily in our days.

CONTENTS

Author's Preface i

PART I:
An Introduction to the Noahide Covenant

1. A Torah Tradition and a Birthright — Not a Religion 1
2. What are the Laws? 3
3. Where is the Spirituality 4
4. The Price of Freedom: Understanding the
   Inflexibility of the Noahide Laws 7
5. Noahide Justice in Proper Perspective: Answering
   the Fear-mongers and Anti-Semites 8
6. A Question of Authority: Trusting *HaShem*'s System
   of Judgment and Establishing it on Earth 14
7. Studying the Seven Laws — A Must for Keeping
   HaShem's Law 20
8. A Simple, Concise Tool for the Initial Study of All
   the Noahide Laws: Understanding this Guide 21

PART II:
The Covenant Of The Seven Commandments
To The Children Of Noah

A. The Seven Noahide Commandments

1. Idolatry 29
2. Cursing a name of God 34
3. Murder 34
4. Forbidden Sexual Intercourse 37
5. Stealing 42
6. Eating Meat Removed from a Living Animal 46
7. Establishing Justice: Enforcing the Law 47

B. Laws Not Included in the Seven Commandments

1. The Prohibitions 50
2. The Obligation of Circumcision for Arabic Peoples 60
3. The Gift of Repentance and the
   'Life of the World to Come' 61
4. Rights of Non-Jews In Torah Law 64
5. Regarding *Geruth Toshav* & Noahide Oaths 71

C. Cases of Exemption From the Noahide Laws & Their Punishment

1. Minors, the Insane, and the Deaf 72
2. Cases of Coercion 73
3. Cases of Doubt 73
4. Cases of Unintentional Transgression 74
5. Conversion to Judaism 74

PART III
Beyond the Letter of the Law:
The Common Decency That *Hashem* Desires of Non-Jews

Introduction to Part III 81
1. Fear of *HaShem*, Hearkening to the Prophet
   Who Speaks in His Name 82
2. Seeking Torah Guidance of the Wise 83
3. Teaching One's Children 85
4. Honoring Parents 87
5. Respect for Women and Modesty 91
6. Marriage & Family versus a 'Planet of the Apes' 96
7. Truthfulness and Repentance 99
8. Honesty and Respect in Marriage 103
9. The Choice between the Pit of Depression
   and a Life of Joy 103
10. Refraining from Cruel Anger 107
11. Kindness and Hospitality 110

12. Blessing, Standing By, and Recognizing the
    Role of the Jewish People 112
13. The Value of Working for One's Sustenance
    and Well-being 119
14. Preserving the Earth and its Species 121

PART IV
Frequently Asked Questions

A. Interacting with Non-Noahides (1-7) 137
B. Ending the Loneliness, Getting Involved (8-10) 141
C. Torah Outlook (11,12) 147
D. Responding to Haters of Israel (13-15) 150
E. Preparing For the Future (16,17) 158
F. Day-to-day Practical *Halakhah* (18-21) 160

Appendix I: Structure of the *Mishneh Torah* 167

Appendix II: *HaShem*'s Incomparable Oneness 173

Appendix III: Refuting Anti-Zionist Torah Scholars 179

About the Author 185

AUTHOR'S PREFACE

Background and History

At Mount Sinai, *HaShem* (God) told the nation of Israel through Moses: *"and you shall be to Me a kingdom of priests, and a holy nation..." (Exodus 19:6)* As the priesthood of mankind, one of the principal roles of the Jewish People — besides serving as a moral example by adhering to our own Covenant with *HaShem* and maintaining His Temple of as a center of worship for all peoples — is *to actually teach the other nations the laws of God that pertain to them*. It is no less an outright Commandment to Moses that Israel bring the entire world to the observance of the Seven Noahide Laws. *(Book of Judges [14th book of Mishneh Torah], Laws of Kings and Wars 8:13[10]. See below for an explanation of Mishneh Torah and its importance. See Appendix I for a complete list of its 14 books and their sections of law.)*

This book was written purely out of the desire to aid in the fulfillment of that Commandment – *to help everyone to know and understand the entire Noahide Covenant: the Noahide so he may keep it properly, and the Jew that he may teach it accurately.*

Over many centuries, the long and bitter conditions of exile — including the great social, philosophical, and spiritual revolutions that swept the world — not only had a marked effect on the way Torah is practiced and taught, but on *what* is practiced and taught. Some obligations were all but forgotten, particularly national obligations on the Jewish People as a whole. **One such obligation was the spread of the observance of the Seven Noahide Laws.**

Thanks to *HaShem*, the miracles of the founding of the state of Israel, the in-gathering of the exiles, and unprecedented Orthodox Jewish outreach to the secular Jewish masses, have all brought about a great restoration of Torah observance. While the ranks of the mainstream Orthodox systems have swelled; smaller schools of thought have emerged as well, working to renew interest in fulfilling the national obligations of the Jewish People, and to restore a truer, more authentic practice of *HaShem*'s Law.

In this current, expansive phase in the history of Jewish thought and practice, *Torah outreach to non-Jews has experienced a rebirth.* In the last forty years, a number of pioneering efforts with many merits have been made in the field of Noahide education. However, until recently, non-Jews still lacked a clear, authoritative legal guide. Left with little awareness of the true nature, breadth and richness of the Torah's legal framework for non-Jews — much less how to study it — they continued to pursue any Torah learning they could find, be it Chabad-style Hassidism for Noahides, or local Kabbalah classes...

The Need of the Hour:
To Teach Rambam According to Rambam

A milestone was reached in 2008, with the publication of *The Divine Code* by Rabbi Moshe Weiner: With the assistance of Rabbi Eliyahu Touger, English translator and commentator to the Moznaim *Mishneh Torah* series, here was a first attempt to produce a comprehensive legal code — a veritable *Shulhhan `Arukh* (a more recent code of Jewish Law written in the 16th century) for Noahides based chiefly on *Mishneh Torah*. *Mishneh Torah* is the great, encyclopedic code of practical Torah law written by **RaMBaM** (**R**abbi **M**oshe **b**en **M**aimon, 1135-1204) of blessed memory. This is greatly significant.

In theory, God's entire Law (including all the laws for non-Jews) can be completely learned, successfully practiced, and taught straight from the ancient, written sources: Bible and the sum total of Talmudic literature, which is the repository of the Oral Law (*Mishnah, Tosefta, Mekhilta, Sifre, Sifra, Jerusalem Talmud,* and *Babylonian Talmud*). Since the Jewish

Sages sealed the Oral Law from further redaction with the completion of the Babylonian Talmud, these sources represent the full court record – an unbroken tradition since Moses at Mt. Sinai – by which we can know every detail of *how* the laws must be kept, and how those details were received, or derived by the Sages from the Written Law, the Bible.

Practically, however, this is very complicated. Many years of intensive study are required to master this vast sea of literature. The final and most authoritative layer of this legal tradition, before it was sealed against later reform, is the Babylonian Talmud. (*Talmud Bavli*) It will henceforth be referred to here as Talmud. It was written in a difficult dialect of Aramaic mixed with other languages. Furthermore, in our times, we no longer have texts of the Talmud that are uncensored and fully accurate. We no longer have the tradition required to identify non-authoritative conclusions added into the Talmud (despite the fact it was to remain sealed) by post-Talmudic sages. We no longer have the ability to accurately distinguish between the authentic traditions received by the *Geonim* — though not included in the Talmud — and their non-authoritative conclusions.

Mishneh Torah is the most accurate, and the only fully-encyclopedic code of Torah Law (relating to the entire Law) ever written, besides the much later and less authoritative *Arukh haShulhhan*. Written 850 years ago, it was written from an earlier and clearer vantage point than subsequent codes of law, shortly after the close of the era of the *Geonim* (the rabbinical sages of the era from after the sealing of the Talmud until the 11th century). Most importantly, the author was a highly critical researcher: Not content even with the commonly-relied-upon Talmudic literature and traditions even in those times (and the inaccurate legal opinions based on them), RaMBaM — one of the greatest masters of Talmud ever — sought out the most reliable manuscripts and consulted the Torah sages in the land of Israel *in his day*. For example, he corrected a common mistake from the rabbis of the Geonic era, based on his discovery of a portion of a retired Talmud written on animal skins, some 500 years old in his day. *(Book of Judgments, Laws of Claimant and Respondent 15:4[2])*

In this aggressive pursuit of truth, RaMBaM wrote the *Mishneh Torah* in order to codify and thereby preserve the most accurate understanding of law possible. An understanding that can only be achieved *by mastering the entire corpus of the primary sources of the Oral Law (the Talmudic literature) from the most reliable sources that existed in his time.* He wrote it in simple, clear Hebrew; making it far easier to master than the ocean of difficult, terse Hebrew and archaic Aramaic, in order to put the entire breadth of Torah Law even in the hands of laymen, women, and children; not only advanced Torah scholars. *For these reasons and more, the best way to learn, practice and teach pure Talmudic law in our times is straight from the Mishneh Torah.*

However, while Rabbi Weiner's groundbreaking work is very much based in RaMBaM's Mishneh Torah and presents the Noahide laws in a digestible format, it is not fully comprehensive. Moreover, rather than presenting the laws simply as they were codified and then restated in Mishneh Torah, the Noahide laws are interpreted in the broader context of Talmudic and post-Talmudic literature – a rabbinical style that is widespread in our times. RaMBaM intended his legal code to be understood as a system unto itself. In his epistle to his favorite student, Rav Yosef ben Yehudah, (1) he wrote:

> I have already warned you not to become lax until you know the entire composition [*Mishneh Torah*], and that it should become your book. And you should learn it everywhere [you go], in order that you may attain its maximum

benefit. *For the intended purpose of what was written in the Talmud and books like it, is already finished and complete.* And the purpose of learning [Talmud] is a waste of time in the Talmud's back and forth argumentation — as if its goal and purpose were for training in debate, and nothing more! And that was not the main goal. Rather, the back and forth argumentation and the debates came about incidentally. When something to be weighed was stated, and someone interpreted it one way, and another interpreted it the opposite; each one was obliged to clarify his way of learning, and to prove his understanding. *And the main goal was nothing but knowing what one must do, and what to avoid.*

If our purpose had been to interpret the composition [Mishneh Torah] by means of the Talmud, we would not have written the work.

In his commentary to the above statement Rav Yosef Qapahh, of blessed memory, clarified the intent of RaMBaM:

This is to say that *the purpose of the give and take and debates and investigations that are in Talmud are totally finished,* according to our Rabbi's [RaMBaM's] opinion. For they did not come about except for the need of the times: to clarify teachings from the *Mishnah* and unclear *Beraithoth* [official teachings from the early, ordained Rabbis that were not included in the *Mishnah*] teachings and even unclarified rationalizations. *But after everything had been elucidated, there is no need to be occupied with them.* And see his Interpretation of the *Mishnah* in Nazir chapter 2, *Mishnah* 1: "Since the teachings of Rabbi Yehudah are in the name of the School of Shammai, and the teachings of the School of Shammai were rejected, *we do not care what they said.*

Mishneh Torah is the only comprehensively written system of authentic Talmudic Noahide Law. Until a true Sanhedrin is restored in Israel, **Noahide scholars require a guide that works within that system with perfectly consistency.** This, alone, can enable Noahides to make decisive legal decisions with confidence. This purist approach to Mishneh Torah was hailed and defended by the famed author of *Shulhhan 'Arukh*, Rav Yoseph Caro (2):

> **Response:** Who is he whose heart conspires to approach forcing congregations who practice according to the RaMBaM of blessed memory, to go by any one of the early or latter-day Torah authorities?! Is it not a case of *a fortiori*, that regarding the School of Shammai — *that the halakhah does not go according to them* — they [the Talmudic Sages] said 'if [one practices] like the School of Shammai [he may do so, but] according to their leniencies and their stringencies.' The RaMBaM, is the greatest of all the Torah authorities, and all the communities of the Land of Israel and the Arab-controlled lands and the West [North Africa] practice according to his word, and accepted him upon themselves as their Chief Rabbi. Whoever practices according to him with his leniencies and his stringencies, why coerce them to budge from him?! (*Avqath Rokhel, Responsum #32 [2]*)

The Authentic Rambam Approach of this Work

A Code of the Seven Laws based on *Mishneh Torah* deserves to be taught strictly according to the will and true Torah outlook of its author. Therefore, with sincere, deep respect for greater scholars who have preceded me in this holy work, trusting in the Eternal One whose Torah even "wisens the simpleton" *(Psalms 19:8)*, I girded my own loins to create a simple, unencumbered, yet as complete as possible a guide for Noahides, rooted exclusively in *Mishneh Torah* and Bible.

(3)

- I cite no differences of opinion, because they detract from the goal: to put all the laws of the Noahide Covenant into the capable hands of God-fearing Noahide scholars.

- What I *do* cite, as much as possible, are the Hebrew sources for every law and teaching in the book *in the text*. The goal is to give the inexperienced reader direct access to the study of the Hebrew sources which were previously closed to him, to prove my position to the experienced scholar.

- I strive for a balance between presenting the laws in a format that is digestible, including explanations of the awesome logic behind the laws; while remaining unapologetically true to the literal meaning of the text.
- Beyond explaining the nuances of the law, I reveal to the reader the awesome logic, deep morality and fairness of the Noahide Laws, with pithy responses to the attacks of fear-mongers and anti-Semites.

- In the third section, listing and explaining core, universal Torah values from Bible which directly involve and relate to Noahides; I strive to reveal the great depth and the lofty moral instruction not readily apparent in various Biblical stories, while remaining as concise and free from burdensome philosophy as possible.

A Second Edition: To Provide Answers for Common Questions of Noahides

There are many basic, essential questions that Noahides have regarding the everyday challenges they face. As much as they may be willing, few rabbis are adequately trained to help. While the First Edition was enjoyed primarily by experienced Torah scholars, it left those practical questions unanswered.

For this edition – with the input and help of Noahide scholars – I created Part IV, a list with 21 of the most common, burning questions Noahides have, with carefully researched answers to each one: How to interact with non-Noahide family and friends in difficult situations, what meat is kosher, how to pray, how to defend the Torah against Christian, Moslem and anti-Israel haters, and much more. It tackles the hard questions about how the Noahide community can best grow, and how it should prepare for increasingly difficult times ahead for Israel and the world.

Our Disclaimer

My hope and prayer are that the work succeeds in conveying how the Noahide Laws, as learned directly according to the clear, simple understanding of the Written Torah and the chief, most complete and authoritative source of the Oral Torah (*Mishneh Torah*) — remain as timely and essential today as they ever did in the distant past.

It must be emphasized that even with this Second Edition, Guide for the Noahide is still a work in progress, as we aspire to create a complete "Mishneh Torah" for the Noahide. As much as we toiled to produce as flawless and clear a Guide as possible, places for improvement will continue to be discovered, warranting a future edition. If any error should be found purely on the basis on Bible, *Mishneh Torah*, objective fact, proper grammar, or there is a problem of clarity, kindly report the problem to the author by email at torathmoshe@gmail.com.

Lastly, as comprehensive as we tried to make this guide, *it was not meant to take the place of a competent rabbi or Torah scholar in the field of Noahide Law.* In case of case of doubt, a competent Torah teacher should be consulted.

A Sign of the Times

Perhaps these are the times that RaMBaM referred to in his precious letter to his foremost student, Rav Yoseph ben haRav Yehudah, the era for which the *Mishneh Torah* – the legal foundation of this guide – was written:

> And all that I've described to you regarding who won't accept it [*Mishneh Torah*] properly, that is only in my generation. However, in future generations, when jealousy and the lust for power will disappear, *all of Israel will subsist* [lit. "we be satiated"] *on it alone, and will abandon all else besides it without a doubt,* except for those who seek something to be involved with all their lives, even though it doesn't achieve a purpose.

Perhaps these are the times to which Rebbe Nahhman of Breslov referred, when he wrote,

> Even though *in the future, when any* halakhah *[law] will need to be known, they will open and delve into the RaMBaM* — even so, however, the book *Guide for the Perplexed* and the philosophical works he composed, are forbidden to peruse. (*Siyahh Sarfei Qodesh*)

May we live to the see the day in our lifetimes, when as Jeremiah foretold, the whole law — in its purity — will be "written on the hearts" of the Jewish people (known perfectly by heart), as it is written:

But this is the covenant that I will make with the house of Israel after those days, saith *HaShem*, I will put My law in their inward parts, and in their heart will I write it; and I will be their God, and they shall be My people. *(Jeremiah 31:32)*

This will serve as a shining light and example to a non-Jewish world restored to the Noahide Covenant.

— Mori (Rabbi) Michael-Shelomo Bar-Ron,
Beth Midrash Ohel Moshe, Ramat Beit Shemesh

NOTES

(1) Iggerot — *Letters by Moshe ben Maimon* (Maimonides): Arabic Original With New Translation and Commentary by Rabbi Joseph KafiH, Mossad haRav Kook, Jerusalem, 5754 / 1994, 172 pp.

(2) Biographical information is from the bibliography of The Artscroll Series© / The Stone Edition: *The Chumash* by Rabbi Nosson Scherman, Mesorah Publications Ltd., Brooklyn, NY, 1995, 1313 pp.

(3) A word about the English translations in this book:

All English translations from Bible in this book are original; yet they bear influence and even include direct borrowings from the JPS Bible based on the electronic text (c) by Larry Nelson posted on *www.mechon-mamre.org*. The translations also bear the influence of *The Living Torah: The Five Books of Moses* by Rabbi Aryeh Kaplan (Maznaim Publishing Corporation, New York, 647 pp.), and The Artscroll Series © / The Stone Edition: *The Chumash*.

All quotes from *Mishneh Torah* were painstakingly translated by the author from the authentic Yemenite manuscript edition posted on the above website. Quotes from Talmud (the Babylonian Talmud) were translated thus as well, from the edition found at the same website. I cannot express enough gratitude to the webmaster of Mechon Mamre for his support and advice on this project. Without his contribution, the resulting work would have been greatly inferior.

PART I

AN INTRODUCTION TO THE NOAHIDE COVENANT

הַלְלוּ אֶת יְהוָה כָּל גּוֹיִם,
שַׁבְּחוּהוּ כָּל הָאֻמִּים.

(תהילים קיז,א)

*Praise YHWH * all peoples,
laud him all the nations*

(Psalms 117,1)

---

*Not to be pronounced. This is read as the holy Name '*Adhonoy*' or the non-sacred term *HaShem*, which means literally "The Name."

A Torah Tradition and a Birthright; Not a Religion

According to sacred Torah tradition, painstakingly preserved over millennia, the Noahide Laws are the terms of *HaShem*'s covenant with Noah after the Flood. Sadly, they were abandoned and largely forgotten. Then, nearly 800 years later, another global cataclysmic event shook the world: the frightening and awesome events coinciding with the Exodus and the Giving of the Torah at Sinai. As I wrote in a recent web article (1):

> In his earth-shaking work, *Worlds In Collision* (2) the late Jewish scientist and Torah scholar Immanuel Velikovsky (despite certain apostate opinions he expresses, which are unnecessary to his thesis, neither adding or diminishing from the strength of his arguments) pieces together a likely scenario for the historical, global Sinai event. Showing the harmony between dozens of traditional sources from every literate culture on earth — from Aztec traditions to the records of the Chinese — that all recall the same time in history, he proves something that would have been difficult for the great rational Sefaradi sages of the Middle Ages to take literally: *When the Yalquth Shim`oni teaches that when the Red Sea split, so did every water body on earth, and when our sages taught that every nation on earth heard the Ten Statements, they were passing down a memory that is shared by all mankind.* According to our tradition *(Bereshith Rabbah)*, the Sinai event was no less than the end of the sixth world age, and the beginning of the seventh.

Since that second rebirth of the world, the nations of the world have been obligated to these laws through the Torah of Moses. After all, it is only through the Torah that mankind even knows the true historical account of the Deluge and *HaShem's* Covenant with Noah. Moreover, it is only through the **Oral Tradition** (preserved by the chain of prophets and ordained rabbis of Israel from Sinai until the completion of the Babylonian Talmud) that the authoritative interpretation of the laws can be known.

This explains why one who fulfills the Noahide Laws specifically because *HaShem* commanded them in the Torah, and informed us through Moses that the nations had been Commanded them originally, is called a *hhassid umoth ha`olam* — a pious one of the nations — and has a special place in the "World to Come", an afterlife of unfathomable spiritual bliss, just as a righteous Israelite does. *(Book of Judges, Laws of Kings and Wars 8:14[11]* — see Appendix I for a list of the books of *Mishneh Torah)* This is as opposed to one who fulfills the Seven Commandments only out of rational thinking. While he is considered a sage of the nations, he is not promised the gift of the afterlife, the "Life of the World to Come."

The term *Ben Noahh* ("son of Noah") as opposed to the generic term *goy* (gentile or non-Jew), refers to one who fulfills the Covenant *HaShem* made with Noah after the Flood. nce the laws of the Jubilee year are restored in the land of Israel, Noahides will once again be entitled to enjoy special rights in Israel as resident aliens, such as free medical care (see Part II, *Rights of Non-Jews in Torah Law*).

The nation of Israel are not called *Bene Noahh*, *(Book of Promising, Laws of Vows 9:21)* since they entered into a distinct Covenant with the Creator at Sinai, after *HaShem* delivered the nation from Egypt. Actually, this separation began gradually with Israel's forefather Abraham, who was sanctified with the additional commandment of circumcision, according to the unique role of the nation that would stem from him — the role of holy priests to minister to the other nations of the world. However, *before the Giving of the Torah at Sinai, the Hebrews had the* halakhic *(legal) status of Noahides.* Fittingly, the Torah's account of their lives and deeds should be understood primarily in the context of the Noahide covenant. They are a perfect case study by which we can identify the behavior *HaShem* desires and demands of mankind, and the behavior He rejects and forbids; that which He rewards, and that for which He admonishes and punishes.

We now see that, unlike Israel's Covenant at Sinai, the Noahide Covenant is not a religion that one must convert to, a people one must be accepted into. *It is the Divinely-ordained legal, social, moral, and spiritual framework that non-Jewish human beings are born into* — just as we are all born into a natural framework of physical laws and limitations. That fits in with the Torah tradition that six of the Seven Laws were already given to Adam in the Garden of Eden. After the Deluge, *HaShem* renewed the Covenant and expanded it to include the new prohibition of meat taken from a living animal.

Beyond the legal definition, it is a birthright — a free gift to anyone born into this world — as the basic moral foundation for a life in harmony with the Creator and other people.

What Are the Laws?

The Noahide Covenant is made of Seven fundamental Commandments, which are generally viewed as Seven categories of Law, containing other laws within them, and other laws that accompany them. The Seven general Commandments — mainly prohibitions — appear in Talmudic literature under the following titles:

> **Idolatry** (prohibition)
> **Cursing a Name of God** (prohibition)
> **Murder** (prohibition)
> **Forbidden sexual relations** (prohibition)
> **Theft** (prohibition)
> **Eating Meat Taken From a Living Animal** (prohibition)
> **Justice** (obligation to enforce the law)

The simplicity of this Covenant is striking. It includes no religious ceremonies, requires no sacrificial service, no priestly hierarchy. Equality between men and women. Equality of all races and colors. What a vision... what a world!

It is the most basic code of human behavior that allows for a world united under the One and Only King of the Universe. Fittingly, it is forbidden, according to Torah, for non-Jews to create man-made religions. Why add to the simple perfection of *HaShem*'s covenant? "You shall not add and you shall not subtract from it." *(Deut. 13:1)* Just as with the rest of the Torah, adding is subtracting. The suffering and death in the name of man-made religion should be enough of a proof to the wisdom of this prohibition!

Where is the Spirituality?

The lack of organized religion is difficult for some. For those who grew up in rich, idolatrous backgrounds with song and ceremony, the six Prohibitions and the single Positive Commandment do not satisfy their spiritual thirst for more. For such people it is important to stress that *the Seven Laws are a beginning — not an end.* With only a few exceptions, a Noahide may practice any of the Torah obligations of a Jew and receive Heavenly reward. Therefore, for those whose souls thirst for more closeness to *HaShem* and to fulfill more of His Torah Commandments, there is tremendous room for growth beyond the Seven. Consider what is written in *Yalquth Shim`oni (Judges, section 42):*

> I bring heaven and earth to witness that the Divine Spirit rests upon a non-Jew as well as upon a Jew, upon a woman as well as upon a man, upon a maidservant as well as a manservant. All depends on the deeds of the particular individual.

However, meriting the Divine Spirit in this relatively short physical life is nothing compared to the eternal spiritual bliss of the 'Life of the World to Come', mentioned above. *When a non-Jew upholds the Seven Commandments for the non-Jew in his/her lifetime, he receives this eternal reward just as the Jew who keeps the 613 Commandments from Sinai.* While it is not on the same level as the much greater yoke of the 613, it is an eternal life for the soul, basking in the radiance of the *Shekhinah*, the Divine Presence. Although there is not a single soul who has seen it and returned to describe it to us, we have a timeless, unbroken Torah tradition that it is a blissful state so sublime, that no earthly joy can remotely compare to it. And the soul that does not merit that life, experiences destruction much greater than that of the body: *the utter death of the soul.*

One need not wait for death to experience the bliss of *devequth* — 'attaching' oneself spiritually to *HaShem*. For example, the Noahide Laws, just as the Torah's Laws, were designed ideally for a world practicing sacrifice of kosher animals to *HaShem*. Kosher whole-burnt offerings were accepted from non-Jews in the First and Second Temples, and will be accepted in the Third Temple to come. But even before we merit this sign of the final redemption, *Noahides may build altars to HaShem and give up offerings today, just as*

Israel's patriarchs Abraham, Issac, and Jacob did. Now the word "sacrifice" just does not do justice to the true meaning of *qorban*, its Hebrew equivalent. *Qorban*, deriving from *qarov*, meaning "close", has no English equivalent. For lack of a better term, we could coin a new term, calling it a "closifier" — something that brings you close to *HaShem*. For one who comes with pure belief and intentions, who is righteous, humble and wholehearted, and has the proper value and respect for the animal (seeing it as representing himself); proper `avodah ('qorban'-service) holds the potential to boost one's spirituality to the level of prophecy, should it be HaShem's Will.*

What is far simpler, more practical and much less costly and difficult is the `avodah she-balev* — the service of the heart: **prayer**. *(Book of Love, Laws of Prayer 1:1)* Again, with pure belief and intentions, the righteous, humble and wholehearted Noahide can pray just as the spiritual masters of Israel prayed throughout the ages: with spontaneous words or in planned, regular prayer (so long as he does not create a new religious rite that is viewed as obligatory, out loud or in quiet meditation, in a proper place of worship or in nature, with the heartfelt tears of casting one's burden on *HaShem*, or with the ecstatic joy and rapture one feels when recounting His praises and recalling His mercies and salvations, remaining motionless or praying through dance... The world of the spirit is as wide open to the righteous Noahide as it is to the righteous Jew. (For recommended reading, see Part II Section B-1g: *What May be Studied*)

However, one must bear in mind that the very foundation of any relationship with the True God is knowing and fulfilling all the precepts that HaShem commanded us as Jews and Noahides, respectively.

The Price Of Freedom:
Understanding The Inflexibility of the Noahide Laws

Again, the Code of the Seven Laws — by which the non-Jew achieves blessing, meaning, and connection with *HaShem* in this world, and the unfathomable bliss of the afterlife — does not include such demanding ritual obligations as circumcision, Sabbath observance of any kind, wearing *tefillin* (phylacteries), or wrapping oneself in a fringed *tallith*-shawl. The Noahide is freed from these obligations, the demanding regimen of holidays and prayers, and more. Although there are a handful of less severe rabbinical obligations, there are no 'rabbinical fences' to Noahide law. *What Noahides are bidden to uphold, is a simple code of the most basic moral elements to human existence.* According to RaMBaM, these can even be arrived at naturally through human logic. *(Laws of Kings and Wars 9:2[1])*

However, being charged to uphold no more than the sheer bedrock of morality by which a human is elevated above the animal, comes with a price: there is no padding or cushioning of protective rabbinical 'fences' around *HaShem's* law for one to break first, causing him to stop before a committing a severe crime... Furthermore, these are not laws given in the framework of any special nation's special, protective, Divine Covenant, with minimal measures beyond which one is exempt, and a justice system that makes capital punishment rare and unusual.

The price, therefore, is an enormous responsibility not to breach them — and great reprehensibility for those who do. Regarding the bedrock Seven laws that almost any mind can arrive at independently, the Torah does not recognize any excuse that can legitimize the *willful* transgression of a Noahide Law; no plea of ignorance. *(Ibid. 10:2[1])* When a person *willfully* transgresses the basic Divine laws that make human life possible, it is a crime against life itself and therefore a *capital crime*. Likewise, as *HaShem's* bedrock principles of morality for humanity, there are no minimal measures beyond which one is exempt: ultimately theft is theft, whether one dollar was stolen from a wealthy man, or a poor man was robbed of all he owned. *(Ibid. 9:12[9])* It could be said from *HaShem*'s perspective, that for the individual, for a community, for a nation, and for the whole world, *observance of the Seven Laws are the price for a human being's right to life.* Clearly, matters of such importance require careful study.

Noahide Justice In Proper Perspective: Answering the Fear-Mongers and Anti-Semites

Sadly, there are those out there with no desire to study honestly, and the issue of capital punishment has become a source for antagonism to the Seven Laws. Anti-semitic literature, written from a place of blind ignorance and hate, cite this as a desire on the part of the rabbis to butcher the gentile world, *HaShem* forbid! The best source I've seen clearing the Talmud Sages of this vicious libel is the website of Rabbi Gil Student, "The Real Truth About the Talmud" *(talmud.faithweb.com).* The following points relate specifically to the Noahide laws:

- In teaching the laws by which one is liable for the death penalty, we are teaching a religious ideal; we are not suggesting that non-Jews carry out Noahide justice today against the law of their local governments.

All live under governments that would incarcerate or even execute anyone who takes the law into their own hands in such a manner. Therefore, except for the ruling elite themselves *(who could, in theory, bring about this change over a period of time, if they were so inclined),* most people are, for all intents and purposes, exempt from this Commandment.

Contrast that with the well-known racist, vigilante violence incited and perpetrated by the white supremacists, neo-Nazis and anti-Semitic Christians who demonize the Talmud and Noahide Laws.

- The most basic purpose of the Torah's laws and teachings: education about what *HaShem* expects of us – that we build a decent world in this life, and inherit the eternal 'life of the World to Come.'

The very word *Torah* literally means "teaching." Fittingly, the Torah, for Jews and for gentiles, is referred to in Proverbs 3:18 as "a tree of life." *The Torah was given primarily in order to educate and uplift us, not to kill us.* Practically speaking, the vast majority of cases are never caught, and in our own day, Western countries do not even enforce a single one of the Seven as they should. Until human nature changes drastically, the Torah must warn us of the proper punishment for these crimes, so that we realize the gravity of these actions that people normally take so lightly. One who transgresses these fundamental laws has violated something so serious, it is as though he has undermined his right to life. This realization should awaken the person to repent properly, so he can live before *HaShem* with a clean slate, and after death be spared the utter destruction of the soul, meriting the eternal reward of the righteous.

But should a society not rectify itself in due time but degenerate past a certain point, *HaShem* Himself will act to mete out its just deserts. It is a matter of question as to how long *HaShem* Himself will tolerate a ruling world order that repudiates the Noahide Laws and persecutes the Jewish People in their homeland.

- According to Torah law; a Jew is liable to the death penalty in a great number of cases (such as a complex list of violations of the Sabbath day) that don't even exist for Noahides.

While it is true that various punishments according to the Seven Laws do not apply equally to Jews; Israelites, in fact, are potentially liable for even more capital offenses that do not even pertain to Noahides. While a Noahide can only be put to death by beheading; punishments under Israel's Covenant at Sinai are more varied and severe, including burning, death by stoning, and strangulation as well. (Although mentioned in Deut. 21:22-23, hanging is not one of the four death penalties, but only done to the already stoned dead body in two cases of Jewish execution: one who curses *HaShem*'s Name and one who worships an idol. [*Book of Judges, Laws of Sanhedrin 15:8-9[6-7]*]).

That is, of course, if he were convicted with proper testimony and fair warning at a time when a true Sanhedrin [Great Court] reigns, and when they sit in the Holy Temple's Chamber of Hewn Stone. But in Israel — except for certain emergency cases — *there can be no capital punishment before the Temple is rebuilt, even after the Sanhedrin is reinstated. (Book of Judges, Laws of Sanhedrin 14:11[10]) And again, rabbis do not even imply, much less instruct modern Noahides to execute Noahide justice in our times and circumstances.*

(**Note:** There is no intention here that Noahides are permitted to remain aloof to their God-given obligation to carry out Noahide justice: The point is that Noahides are generally neither encouraged nor expected to break the laws of their land and be punished for doing so. Unlike Israel, the Noahide is not obligated to sanctify *HaShem*'s Name (*Qidush HaShem*). We encourage Noahides to call for legislative changes that push their respective governments ever closer to compliance with all the Noahide laws.)

- In authentic Torah law, Jews who spitefully reject their covenant are generally considered lower than non-Jewish idolaters. (*Book of Judges, Laws of Witnesses 11:11[10]*)

In fact, there is — under narrow, tightly-defined criteria — a unique Torah judgment against a Jewish city in Israel that was seduced to idolatry. *(Book of Knowledge, Laws of Idolatry ch.4)* After all the idolaters in it are brought to justice, the city is burned down and forbidden to ever be rebuilt. *No such judgment exists for gentile city that was seduced to idolatry.*

Moreover, by means of conversion, blessed Israelite status is open to any sincere, God-fearing human being on earth. Clearly, unlike the way it is commonly portrayed, the Torah is not racist against any people. But what about whole peoples that the Torah punishes in its laws — Amalek, Ammon, Moab, Edom, and Egypt? Those nations freely chose to commit crimes that became their legacy. Moreover, because the world's peoples have mixed thoroughly; according to practical Torah law today, *no one today has the halakhic judgment of a member of any of those peoples. (Book of Holiness, Laws of Forbidden Sexual Relations 12:19-20[25])*

- It is expressly taught in *Mishneh Torah* — the ultimate Code of Jewish Law — that tyrannizing other peoples is not a goal of the Jewish People, not now or ever.

According to our Divine mandate, the purpose of the Jewish people is to sanctify the Name of *HaShem* in this world by the fulfilling His Commandments. *(Book of Knowledge, Laws of the Foundations of Torah 5:1)* Our desire is to be free to delve as deeply into Torah and know *HaShem* to the extent we are able — not to lord over anyone. As the RaMBaM teaches:

> *The prophets and sages did not longingly desire the days of the Messiah in order to rule the entire world, and not in order to tyrannize the gentiles, and not so that the peoples would raise them up as rulers,* and not in order to eat, drink, or enjoy

> themselves; but rather, so that they would be free for [the study of] Torah and its wisdom, and they would have no taskmaster or disturbance, in order that they should merit the life of the World to Come... *(Book of Judges, Laws of Kings and Wars 12:7[4])*

> *Those who slander the Noahide Laws comfortably ignore the breadth of the Oral Law, which is saturated with teachings of peace and goodwill towards idolaters. The Oral Law is protective of property and welfare of gentiles to the extent that stealing from an idolater is considered worse than stealing from a Jew!* (RaMBaM's Commentary to the *Mishnah, tractate Kelim 12:7)*

Most if not all the above-mentioned hate groups would do well to preach to the mirror. As white supremacists and neo-Nazis, they incite violence against innocents and identify with those who committed the worst genocide in known history. What Jewish or Jewish-aligned group ever perpetrated such crimes? They neither understand, nor do they care about the proper context of these laws.

Such slanderers conveniently ignore that outside of Israel, these laws were intended to be adjudicated by non-Jews in their own courts: not by Jewish courts or Jewish judges.

Justice for non-Jewish communities is their own responsibility and obligation — not anyone else's.

For those who cannot imagine how society could feasibly be so greatly transformed, consider the following. When Israel came out of Egypt, they were almost totally assimilated into the idolatry of Egypt. But *HaShem* led the people of Israel through a 40-year process of transformation to its unique God-given system of government Before entering the Land, where all the Commandments would be in force. It is reasonable to assume that, by the legislative enactment of a true Sanhedrin in Israel, an *entire society that adopts the Noahide Covenant could be allowed a gradual process of transformation to national life according to the Seven Laws.*

- Beyond the wisdom, beauty and fairness of the Noahide Laws (however abrasive they may be to currently widespread notions of political correctness) they need not impress: They must ultimately be accepted because they are Torah Law, according to the Oral Tradition.

Those who reject the Noahide Laws invariably reject the Oral Law to begin with. They imagine the ancient Rabbis to have been corrupt legislators who added laws against the Torah prohibition to do so *(Deut 13:1) – God forbid*. They imagine that such rabbinical legislation came to replace an original, purer, "biblical" Judaism.

To refute such nonsense, I refer the reader to my soon-to-be-published work, *Eighteen Proofs of the Authenticity of the Oral Torah Tradition* (© Lightcatcher Books, 2010). I offer proofs from the Bible, other ancient literature, archaeology, and ethnic studies to establish the deep antiquity, biblical authenticity, and Divine sanction of the Oral Law. The reader is shown how, beginning with the first Court of 70 elders ordained by Moses, *HaShem* appointed the Great Court *(the Sanhedrin)* to be the bastion of an unbroken Oral Tradition from Sinai. In the Written Torah, God Himself establishes their authority **in every generation.** That includes the authority to enact original decrees in their own name (lacking the same force as God's original 613 Commandments) – a power we see exercised and recognized by God and the prophets in the Bible itself. *It is impossible for Jew or non-Jew to fulfill the written Word of God except according to that oral body of instruction.*

In the days of Rabbi Judah the Prince (2nd century C.E.), the ordained Sages of Israel were forced by circumstance to create an official, written court record of the Oral tradition. They produced the *Mishnah*, which recorded the authoritative traditions, interpretations, and rulings of Israel's ordained sages since the 70 elders under Moses at Sinai until their day. *(Introduction to M.T. [Mishneh Torah] 12-15)* Thus began a process by which ordained sages of each generation – both in Israel and Babylonia – would expound on the *Mishnah*, record other authoritative traditions, and further clarify the Law. As explained in the Preface, the process was complete with the sealing of the Babylonian Talmud (circa 500 C.E.). *(Ibid. 32-34)* The Talmudic literature remains the final repository of the legal traditions of the last Sanhedrin. Thanks to the tireless efforts of those Sages over the span of three centuries, the authentic Oral Law of Moses is in our hands today, well intact.

A Question of Authority: Trusting *Hashem's* System of Judgment, Establishing It Here on Earth

People with little Torah knowledge cannot be fully aware of the steep moral character requirements of a Torah judge, how much more so a member of the Great Court, the Sanhedrin. They know nothing of his legendary fear of *HaShem* and undying loyalty to upholding God's true Word. In fact, these are precisely two of the required traits of Torah judges in the Written Word:

> *Moreover you shall seek out of all the people men of valor who fear God, men of truth – hating unjust gain;* and place such over them, to be rulers of thousands, rulers of hundreds, rulers of fifties, and rulers of tens. (Jethro's words to Moses in *Ex. 18:19-22*. See where *HaShem* Commands Moses thus in *Num. 11:16-17*)

After summarizing the full meaning of the Torah's terse wording, RaMBaM describes the selection process the Sages employed:

> The Sages said that from the Great Court, they would send agents throughout the Land of Israel and check. Whomever they would find to be *wise, God-fearing, humble, discerning, mature, and amicable* – they would make him a judge in his town. And from there they would advance him to [the court at] the entrance of the Temple Mount, and from there they would advance him up to [the court at] the entrance to the Temple Courtyard, and from there they would advance him up to the Great Court. *(Laws of the Sanhedrin... 2:11[8])*

All the above is besides the knowledge, both Torah and secular (such as mastery of foreign languages), physical fitness and normal appearance that are required of a Torah judge. (*Laws of the Sanhedrin...*)

Clearly Israel's Great Court justices were not, like so many governments throughout history, run by entrenched, corrupt political families. They were carefully selected from all of Israel based on both wisdom and moral virtue. This is how men of lowly birth – a woodcutter from Babylonia such as Hillel, an ignorant farmer boy as Eliezer ben Hyrcanus, a poor, ignorant shepherd as Akiva ben Joseph (Rabbi Akiva) – could rise through diligent growth in Torah to become the greatest sages of their respective generations. The Sanhedrin represented the most virtuous men of the nation.

In fact, the Torah clearly shows the notion of Israel's leadership as cruel, blood-thirsty killers to be an affront to *HaShem* Himself. When the newly-freed tribes of Israel that left Egypt lost faith in their human leadership, they forfeited their Divine protection: they were immediately attacked by

Amalek. *(Exodus ch.17)* Later, when a group of Israelites began promulgating lies about Israel's leadership *(Numbers 16:3, 16:14)* — namely that Moses was acting as a mere demagogue — HaShem's response was swift and frightening. A geophysical phenomenon occurred that never was before, and will never be again: the earth fissured open underneath them, swallowing the perpetrators and everything they owned. *(Numbers 16:12-14)* By Divine decree, the stubborn, faithless generation that believed their lies would perish in the desert. And the same children they feared would die in the desert would be the ones to enter the holy land and enjoy its bounty. *(Numbers 14:28-32)* The lesson: *HaShem demands of His People our faith in authentic Heavenly-sanctioned, Torah leadership.*

Of course, Israel — being HaShem's designated nation of priests, the example to the rest of mankind — is 'kept on a short leash.' In war, merely refusing to march is an act of treason for a soldier in a standing army. However, on a basic level, the same lesson is true for all humanity, and the nations would be wise to learn from it. *Non-Jewish nations, too, are expected to appoint and respect their own true Torah leadership: HaShem-fearing Noahide judges, fluent in Noahide Law, who can execute justice according to the Seven Laws.* And they would be wise to appoint such leaders based on the same moral criteria by which Jewish judges are to be appointed.

Consider the bygone nations who failed in this: Sodom and Gomorrah, Egypt, Babylonia, Persia, Sparta, Greece, Pompey, Imperial Rome, Celtic Northern Europe, Aztec Mexico, the Catholic empires of Spain and Portugal that once spanned the Atlantic, the Ottoman Empire (authors of the Armenian genocide), fascist Germany, fascist Italy, fascist imperial Japan, and Communist Russia. Every one of these 'reigns of terror' was notorious for its unbridled cruelty to innocents; nearly all of them for the sexual depravity of its elite... After all, with no belief in the true God, the elite fancy that all is permitted...

However, we must confront all those around us who don't accept the zealous God of the Bible, Who punishes those with lack of faithfulness to His laws. Perhaps they feel their choice not to believe gives them a certain power over reality. It is the childish notion that their choice to believe or not to believe, somehow affects the reality of what *HaShem* demands of us. I haven't found a more poignant and poetic a response than the Book of Job: *Who are we humans to have the audacity to judge the Creator of all existence, being as short-lived, ignorant, myopic and prejudiced as we are?*

Many of those who are comfortable with the idea of "God", actually have the Christian "God is love" equation in mind. They relate to *HaShem* as "The Holy Butler" expected to serve *them*. He is expected to bless them with health, prosperity and answer them in their hour of need — regardless of how they observe His Laws. As He patiently waits for them to wake up, giving them decades of free choice in peace and prosperity; they take this for a sign that all is well, that they are doing what is required. Then, when *HaShem* "fails to perform" and terrible hardship strikes, they either (a) reject religion altogether, (b) blame anything and anyone else (such as the Jews), or (c) absorb the blow mindlessly, without earnestly undertaking to learn the Divine message. That may require a search outside of one's own religion or value system... *unthinkable.*

The alternative to their narrow, Christianized, humanist worldview is too frightening to consider: a Creator with just and wise demands on his Creations for their own good, who is ready to rain down destruction on those who — generation after generation — reject His Laws... laws borrowed by the other main religions... the Torah of the Jews.

Noted Noahide scholar, author and lecturer, James D. Long, regularly uses the following allegory to help people understand and trust in *HaShem*'s justice — which can be harsh at times:

> Imagine if you built a house for guests to stay and partake of your generosity, that they might become better human beings. You give them a few basic rules to ensure their well-being, and that they not forget the purpose for which they are there. What would you do if a guest who had taken up residence in your home, one day armed himself, then began denying your ownership of the home, and then began stealing and even murdering fellow guests and would not leave? *HaShem* built such a 'house', a world, for his guests, His Creations. *Woe to those guests who not only threaten the well-being of their fellow guests, but strive to uproot the very moral purpose for which the house was built!* (from private correspondence)

Perhaps people could more easily come to terms with their responsibility to uphold and live by HaShem's laws — even the rabbinical decrees — if there were a clear human authority to give the final, definitive interpretation. After all, without an ultimate, righteous human arbiter — a Torah authority recognizable and respectable to all — there would be endless internal bickering and discord. The notion of Noahide Law as an instrument of *HaShem*'s kindness would elude many. How else could crime between nations be judged fairly, and grievances settled?

Torah is compared to medicine (*Exodus 15:26*). Any application of the Law in the wrong hands is like a scalpel in the hands of an untrained fool in the operating room! It is for this reason that, in his infinite Wisdom, *HaShem* entrusted the rules of application and ultimate interpretation of the Seven Laws (like the 613 Laws of the Torah), into the hands of the "surgeons" of the Torah — the only judicial institution sanctioned by *HaShem* Himself: the Great Court of 71 ordained rabbinical sages, the Great Sanhedrin of Israel. *(Deut. 16:18, cf. Book of Judges, Laws of Sanhedrin ch.1, and Deut. 17:8-13 cf. Laws of Rebels ch.1)*

When a true Sanhedrin with full *halakhic* (legal) status will eventually be restored in Israel — may we see this day in our lives — it will have the monumental task of determining the precise application of the Noahide Laws in this 58th (21st) century. When that happens, the full vision of Isaiah 2:2-4 will not be far off:

> And it shall come to pass in the end of days, that the mountain of *HaShem*'s house will be established as the top of the mountains, and will be exalted above the hills; and all nations will stream to it. And many peoples will go and say: 'Come and let us go up to the mountain of *HaShem*, to the house of the God of Jacob; and He will teach us of His ways, and we will walk in His paths.' *For out of Zion shall go forth the law, and the word of HaShem from Jerusalem.*

According to sacred Oral Torah tradition, *HaShem*'s teachings going forth from "*HaShem*'s house" refers to the holy judgment of the Sanhedrin, the "Pillar of Teaching" (*Laws of Rebels ch.1*), when they will sit in the Chamber of Hewn Stone in the Temple. May we live to see the prophesied result of their selfless work of righteous judgment:

> And they shall beat their swords into plowshares, and their spears into pruning hooks; nation shall not lift up sword against nation, neither shall they learn war any more. *(Isaiah 2:4)*

For that reason, I suggest that Noahides should — for their own benefit as much as that of the Jewish People — act as a strong external force promoting the establishment of a true Sanhedrin according to *halakhah* (law).

Studying the Seven Laws:
A Practical Must For Keeping God's Law

As mentioned above, careful Noahide observance requires study. *Today, any non-Jew with proper guidance can learn and practice the Seven Laws from the Mishneh Torah of Maimonides.* This unique code of law — the only truly encyclopedic code of Torah Law ever written, and consistently loyal to the final legal rulings recorded in the authoritative Talmudic literature — is a summary of the entire Oral Tradition, including the Seven Laws of Noah.

The Noahide Laws are summarized in the *Book of Judges*, in chapters nine and ten of *Laws of Kings and Wars*, followed by the chapters relating to the Messiah and the prophesied "End of Days." However, there are laws throughout *Mishneh Torah* that are very important for Noahides to study, such as *Laws of the Foundations of Torah*, *Laws of Idol Worship*, and *Laws of Repentance*. These are all found in the first book, *The Book of Knowledge*. From this source, most any diligent human being who applies him or herself properly can learn the most succinct, true and authentic Torah perspective on the most basic principles of faith — without the filter of modernity. Another example is the *Book of Damages*, containing key information on the complex subject of theft. Most of these laws are no less binding on Noahides than on Jews. (Again, for a full list of the books and legal sections of *Mishneh Torah*, see *Appendix I*.)

When these subjects become more familiar and important to people from every race in every land, the world will progress towards the day, when "they shall not hurt nor destroy in all My holy mountain; for the earth will be full of the knowledge of *HaShem*, as the waters cover the sea." *(Isaiah 11:9)*

Sadly, there is a major language barrier to understanding *Mishneh Torah* in the essential, authentic Hebrew. No translation truly does it justice. Even the dedicated few who reach the required proficiency in Hebrew face another problem: Until one acquires encyclopedic knowledge of the 1,000 chapters of its 14 books, it is nearly impossible to understand the full meaning and proper context of the Noahide Laws when they are presented, since they are largely presented as a list of caveats or exceptions to topics which were already previously explained in the *Mishneh Torah* — not as complete explanations in themselves.

A Simple, Concise Tool for the Initial Study of All the Noahide Laws

Therefore, as explained in the Preface, trusting in the Eternal One whose Torah even 'wisens the simpleton' *(Psalms 19:8)*, I endeavored to make a short, concise, yet as complete as possible a summary of all the Noahide Laws: the Seven as well as the rabbinical injunctions required of all non-Jews. I even suggest a few of their major ramifications in the modern world. I aim for a balance between remaining unapologetically true to the letter of the law, while revealing its logic and moral wisdom. *Clearly, this is no easy task in a world largely educated according to Christianized and secular humanist values, and rapidly progressing Islamic influence.*

Beyond the legal obligations, I have listed the principal core values and character traits taught in the Bible that directly involve and relate to Noahides (non-Jews and Israelites before the Giving of the Torah). Although they are not tenets of the Law; historically, Noahides who fulfilled them were raised up high while those who transgressed them were brought down low.

This Guide was not meant to replace serious scholarship of *Mishneh Torah* in the original Hebrew, but *to give as solid and complete as possible a base for non-Jews to understand what truly obligates them under HaShem, what does not, and beyond that the eternal values by which he or she should live.* The underlying purposes are (a) to present the laws in a format that is at once digestible, yet as unapologetically true to *Mishneh Torah* and Bible as possible, and (b) to show how, like all the Laws of the Torah, the Noahide Laws in their simple purity remain as timely and essential today as they ever did in the distant past.

NOTES

(1) Bar-Ron, Michael S. "Revealing the Secret of the Parah Adumah and the Mountain Over Our Heads." A web article at *The Ohel Moshe Society*, found at: *www.torathmoshe.com*

(2) Velikovsky, Immanuel, *Ages in Chaos*, Buccaneer Books, New York 1950. 401 pp.

PART II

THE COVENANT OF THE SEVEN COMMANDMENTS TO THE CHILDREN OF NOAH

Except for the Laws of Slaves (*avadim*) and Resident Aliens in the Land of Israel (*gere toshav*)

אִמְרוּ בַגּוֹיִם יְהוָה מָלָךְ
אַף תִּכּוֹן תֵּבֵל בַּל תִּמּוֹט,
יָדִין עַמִּים בְּמֵישָׁרִים.

(עז, י תהילים)

Say among the nations 'YHWH* reigns' — Even the earth is established that it cannot be moved; He will judge the peoples with equity.

Psalms 96,10

---

* Not to be pronounced. This is read as the holy Name *Adhonoy* or the non-sacred term *HaShem,* which means literally "The Name."

A
The Seven Noahide Commandments

*Further discussion separated by * * * and ending with * * **

KEY TO DEFINITIONS USED:

Noahide (*ben Noahh*) refers to a non-Jew who abides by the Seven Noahide Laws, especially one who does so because of the Torah given at Sinai.

Idolater (`oved `avodah zarah) should ordinarily refer to anyone, Jew or gentile, who serves idolatry. In this book it refers to any non-Jew who is not yet a Noahide *(go)*. *(Note: While "goy" is often an exclusive term in M.T. Torah for an idolater, in certain places it clearly refers to all non-Jews, including Noahides.)*

Non-Jew or Non-Israelite refer to both Noahides and idolaters. Unless otherwise stated, all the laws discussed in this book are in the context of non-Jews. All general terms such as **"one"**, **"a person"**, etc, refer to non-Jews.

Jew, Jewess, or Israelite ordinarily refer to any one born of a Jewish mother or one who was converted properly to Torah Judaism. *In this book, however, it refers to one with the actual legal status of Israelite ('Yisrael'), according to halakhah (applied Torah law).* While this basic status does not require that one appear outwardly religious or even particularly righteous; it *does* require that the Jew be known to espouse the minimal tenets of faith, and to neither worship idols nor publicly violate the Sabbath laws. *(Laws of Idolatry 2:9, Laws of the Sabbath 30:15, Laws of Eruvin 2:16, Laws of Slaughter 4:11[14], etc.) This could be significant in the rights of a Jew in a Torah court case with a non-Jew.*

This distinction proves a critical point: Despite the way it is commonly portrayed, *the Torah is not racist.* *Just as the status of "Noahide" is not an automatic given, but rather a status earned through basic adherence to God's, such is Israelite status.* As mentioned above, authentic Torah views certain biological Jews who spitefully reject their covenant as lower than non-Jewish idolaters. *(Book of Judges, Laws of Witnesses 11:11[10])* At the same time, by means of conversion, blessed Israelite status is open to any sincere, God-fearing human being on earth.

One key difference, of course, is that — *unlike non-Jews* — *it is the right and privilege of any born Jew to live as a halakhic Israelite with no need for conversion.* The law is compassionate towards Jews who were raised in the manner of non-Jews. *(Book of Judges, Laws of Rebels 3:3)* Even a Jew who was raised properly but fell out of observance – except for in certain extreme cases – can repent and automatically regain his status as *Yisrael.*

REGARDING CAPITAL PUNISHMENT:

As stated in Part I, any mention in these laws of capital punishment (the death penalty), *is strictly in the context of a society that is governed according to the Noahide Laws.* Not a single country on earth permits the execution of justice according to these laws; one who does so risks imprisonment or the death penalty himself. Until these laws can be administered under the sanction of law, removing the great personal risk, non-Jews (except for the governing authorities themselves) are exempt from this obligation. Rather, one should focus on the greater loss of committing these sins without repenting: *loss of one's eternal reward* — *the 'Life of the World to Come.'* According to Oral Tradition, a soul that is cut off from the afterlife is utterly destroyed. *(Book of Knowledge, Laws of Repentance 8:2)*

1
Idolatry

Not to worship any created thing (which thereby becomes an idol), be it material or spiritual, live or inanimate, mundane or celestial. This includes any human being, however holy one may believe him to be, such as the ancient kings of Egypt or Jesus. This entails performing one of the four classical devotions of (a) prostrating, (b) lighting incense, (c) pouring out a libation, or (d) sacrificing to an idol. It also entails praying to the idol or practicing any special prescribed rite of religious devotion for it. *(Book of Knowledge, Laws of Idolatry 2:1, 3:1-6)*

- This includes serving the idol (by the above means) as an "officer" of the One, True Creator — as if that makes it fitting to be honored (just like the officers of earthly kings, who are to be honored by the king's own command). It also includes *worshipping the idol as an intermediary or agent between oneself and the One, True Creator of the Universe. (Ibid. 2:2)*

* * * *Sadly, the practice of praying to a deceased saint or Grand Rabbi that he pray on one's behalf, or convey one's prayers to the Almighty, has become more common among certain Hasidic and mystical Sephardic Jews over the last two centuries. These individuals are a dangerous example to Jews and non-Jews everywhere. Although they may defend their practice based on an isolated legend in the Talmud, or because this has already become traditional practice in their community for centuries, these are no proofs at all. The foundation of God's Law for humanity will not be uprooted through such reasoning; they cannot cover up the fact they are playing with fire.* * * *

According to authentic Torah, we are *HaShem's* children, and He desires our prayers as a caring Father. Fittingly, we have no alternative but to pray to him directly with no intermediary. This is known to true Hasidic masters and teachers, such as the Grand Rebbe of Biale Ostrova in Jerusalem, who teaches that one may only pray in the merit of the deceased – never to request anything of them, much less pray to them.

- This also includes *serving the idol as if it were attached, included within, or as a part of the One, True Creator of the Universe.* This has major implications for any religion, cult or sect that serves a plurality of deities, imagining that they are truly parts or different reflections of the One True LORD. Classical Hinduism and Christianity, for example, are idolatry. *(Ibid 2:2, 9:4)*

* * * *HaShem being "One" does not merely imply a singular entity, rather than two or more. Rather it is a Oneness that is beyond comprehension. He is so One, that — unlike physical creatures as ourselves, or even the metaphysical angels — HaShem Himself, His Life, and His Knowledge are utterly one in every aspect, on every plane.* * * *

Otherwise, there would have been three divinities: He, His Life, and His Knowledge. It is said that 'He is the Knower, He is the Known, and He is the Knowledge' — all are perfectly one. Fittingly *HaShem* is the only One to know His True Self, not even the highest archangels. Therefore, unlike we, who know His creations by external knowledge to ourselves; *HaShem* knows them all because of Himself. Therefore, because He knows Himself, He knows everything, for the existence of everything depends utterly on Him. *(Book of Knowledge, Laws of the Foundations of Torah 2:13-15[10]).*

Clearly this is not merely a "unity" of composite parts, but perfect Oneness in every sense. There are neither the words to fully express this, nor is there any intellect that can comprehend it fully.

What we can understand is that — as opposed to the simplistic understanding of various mystical doctrines — *HaShem does not physically fill the Creation; He Himself is not personally "everywhere, inhabiting all things."* If so, HaShem would be divided into parts — the "part of Him" in me and the "part of Him" in you. Moreover, one would be forced to imagine *HaShem* personally inhabiting filth and feces. Neither is the simplistic understanding of the opposite mystical doctrine of *SimSum* (or *tzimtzum*) any more tenable: the notion that God had to "retract within Himself" in order to make room for the universe. This could impart to *HaShem* some semblance of corporeality (physicality), as if He takes up space on some level. *The truth is that HaShem, having no body and with limitless power, does not take up space in any way; space does not apply to Him. What fills all creation is His power and might*, according to the blessing when one hears thunder or other geo-physical and astronomical phenomena *"whose **power** fills the universe." (Book of Love, Laws of Blessings 10:16[14])*

This is easier to accept when one realizes that space and time are God's creations no less than matter and energy. He is clearly beyond the concept of space, and outside of time – in spite of the fact that He interacts with His creations within the time and space, which He created for them.

King Solomon referred to this, when he exclaimed, "But will God really dwell on the earth? Behold, heaven and even the highest heavens cannot contain You – how much less this house that I have built!" *(I Kings 8:27)* Yet *HaShem* is mentioned in no uncertain terms as "sitting" or "dwelling" on earth. Clearly, if the entire universe cannot contain *HaShem*, this "dwelling" is allegorical. We see that physical space does not apply to *HaShem*.

Verses that tell of *HaShem* "dwelling" in a physical place on earth refer to the fact that *HaShem* would make His Divine Presence *(Shekhinah)* known to man in that place. This would generate physical phenomena (cloud, fire, etc.), which cause man to understand that He had invested His attention and concentrated His attention towards that place. This is how *HaShem* would 'dwell' *(yoshev)* between the angelic figures atop the Ark of the Covenant. *(Kings II 19:15) Similarly, all other references in the Bible to HaShem's ways and actions in human terms such as "beneath His feet" (Ex. 24:10); "written by the finger of God" (Ex. 31:18); "the hand of HaShem" (Ex. 9:3, Numbers 11:23, Deut. 2:15); "the eyes of HaShem" (Deut. 11:12); "the ears of HaShem" (Numbers 11:1) and the like were written thus in order to describe HaShem's involvement in the world in simplistic terms that are understandable to all. (Laws of the Foundations of Torah 1:9)*

Moreover, we can clearly see that there is no room in authentic Torah belief for a tripartite divinity (according to the Christian doctrine of "Trinity") or a ten-part divinity (according to pseudo-kabbalistic doctrine (1), or any other product of man's imagination. *Whoever worships such a god is worshiping a foreign deity;* not the God of Israel, eternal Creator and King of the Universe.

(See Appendix II: *Understanding the Oral Tradition of HaShem's Incomparable Oneness*) * * *

However, one is only liable for the death penalty for doing these acts after taking the idol upon oneself as a god (or as an attachment or an inclusive part of the One True God). There are acts of sheer idolatry that are not punishable by death — neither for a Noahide, nor for an Israelite for that matter. *(Laws of Idolatry 9:4)* They include:

1. Sheer idolatry (the classical devotions mentioned above or the idol's prescribed devotional rites) without having accepted the idol as a god, but rather *out of love* for the idol's craftsmanship, or *out of superstitious fear*, lest it harm him. Although strictly forbidden, the transgressor is not liable to the death penalty.

2. Honoring an idol with various acts of respect that are not expressly mentioned in the Torah prohibition (unless the act is a prescribed rite of religious devotion for that particular idol). This includes embracing, kissing, or anointing an idol, dressing or putting shoes on it, sweeping or sprinkling the ground before it or anything of the sort. Nevertheless, these acts are idolatry, and thus strictly forbidden. *Moreover, if any of these simple acts of respect were its prescribed rite of religious devotion, he is liable. (Ibid 3:11-12[6])*

What Does Not Constitute Idolatry

- *Belonging to a particular religious group in name only.* Although certain religions can be directly associated with idolatry; honest conversations with those who are nominally Christian, Buddhist, even Hindu, etc, often reveal that they actually have the beliefs of righteous Noahides. Just as being recognized as an Orthodox Jew does not whitewash an Israelite for committing idolatry, neither does a Noahide being nominally associated with an idolatrous religion make him liable for idolatry.

   * * * That being said, since those who associate with a religion are assumed to accept its beliefs and practice its devotional rites, and being that it was forbidden to invent those religions to begin with: It is important that Noahides of all backgrounds make an effort to shed their idolatrous costume; to gather together and unify, to strengthen one another, and act as a force of goodness in the world. * * *

- *Lust for money, sexual intercourse, and infatuation with "larger than life" culture icons* (i.e. sports or pop personalities). These are objects of widespread obsession among youth in our times — a trend that can resemble idolatrous behavior. However, these vile, unhealthy societal trends are not the idolatry punishable by the Noahide laws: only the performance of special rites and devotions as detailed above.

2
Cursing A Name Of God

Not to curse the Creator, the Sustainer of all existence, by any name referring to Him in any language. This need not be any of the sacred Hebrew names, but even cursing Him by the names "God" or "Allah." *(Laws of Idolatry 9:5[3])*

However, the judgment of one who curses foreign names of HaShem depends on his intention. The capital crime of cursing is only when the intention is towards the One, invisible, undivisible Creator and King of all that exists. There is an opinion that the name *Allah* — rather than a cognate of the holy Hebrew name of God, *Eloah* (one of the seven sacred names of God in Hebrew that may not be erased *[Laws of the Foundations...6:1-2]*) — is actually derived from the name of the ancient Babylonian moon goddess. (2) If one relates to the name *Allah* accordingly, as referring to an idol, there is no prohibition in cursing it.

Fittingly, however unlikely this case may be; if one were to curse the name God with no any intention towards the true Creator, but only towards the original false deity that bore that name *(Isaiah 65:11)*, there would be no punishment. *The intention of the one who curses must be verified.*

3
Murder

Not to murder, commit suicide, or even to abort an unborn human fetus that is 40 or more days old from conception. (This distinction between before and after 40 days from conception is derived from *Book of Sacrifices, Laws of the First-Born 4:11[12] and Book of Seeds, Laws of Heaven Offerings 8:2[3]*)

- *All degrees of murder are included in this prohibition:* Even killing a severely-wounded person *who is about to die*, even by indirect means — such as by putting the victim in the path of destruction, or by leaving the person to starve. *(Laws of Idolatry 9:6[4])*

- *Medical murder:* The prohibition includes criminal cases of actively preventing medical treatment – when it is in good supply — that would definitely save someone in case of a medical emergency that presents a certain, direct, threat to life. This would be the case for a hospital that coldly chooses to end the life of certain patients in order to cut costs; not due to lack of personnel or medicine. It would not be the case for doctors handling mass casualties with limited supplies and personnel. In those trying circumstances, doctors must understandably make difficult decisions as to who has the best chances of being saved through their efforts, and who does not.

- *Killing an enemy to save one's own life, one's city, or one's country* (such as in war) or the lives of others who are targeted victims, is *not included* in this prohibition, *since **not** killing in this case is comparable to (but does not equate) suicide and murder.* Furthermore a non-Jew is exempt from the Noahide laws in a case of risk to their own lives. (see Section C: *"Cases of Exemption from the Noahide Laws"*)

However, a non-Jew who kills for the sake of revenge or by disproportionate use of force (see below) is liable for murder – whether he acts on his own behalf, or as a soldier following orders so that he does not go to jail.

- *Disproportionate use of force* is specifically mentioned in the law. A non-Jew with the ability and means to disable an attacker without killing him (such as by striking one of his limbs), is liable if he strikes the attacker so that he dies. *(Laws of King and Wars 9:6[4])*

* * * *From the Torah's account of lives of the patriarchs Abraham, Isaac and Jacob — especially in light of the Oral traditions — we learn two values. In their lives they give us classical examples of warriorship for the sake of Heaven (i.e. the war on Shechem and other wars with the Amorites). We learn here that taking human life can, under the circumstances, be an act of justice. On the other hand, we see their great self control.*

When Sarah the matriarch was effectively kidnapped by the Pharoah, Abraham the holy warlord — having entering Egypt "with 318 captains under him and an immense army under each of them" — preferred to rely on HaShem's help before resorting to force, risking unnecessary bloodshed. (3) According to oral tradition taught by Rashi, this was the approach of Jacob as well. (4) Although he prepared for war in anticipation of his meeting with Esau upon his return to his homeland; he did his utmost to avoid bloodshed by initially attempting peaceful strategies. * * *

- To my personal understanding, abortion would only be permitted after 40 days (before which it is not forbidden) if the continuation of the pregnancy presents a certain and direct physical, existential threat to the mother's life. *That is because in an extreme case, preventing her from the medical treatment to save her life — which is abortion in this case — could be likened to murder. On her part, she would be fully justified because a non-Jew is exempt from the Noahide laws in a case of risk to their own lives.* (see section III: *Cases of Exemption from the Noahide Laws*)

4
Forbidden Sexual Intercourse

This capital crime specifically includes bestiality, homosexual anal intercourse between males, adultery and incest.

For Noahides, the crime of forbidden intercourse is for vaginal and anal intercourse only — not oral. *(Book of Judges, Laws of Kings and Wars 9:9[7])*

Considering the technical definitions of capital crimes of forbidden sexual intercourse, it is perfectly clear that — in regards to homosexuality — *it is the act of forbidden intercourse that makes one liable; not one's sexual orientation.* Nothing in the Written Torah or Oral tradition implies that those of the homosexual persuasion are held liable in heaven or on earth for their orientation – the feelings in their heart.

* * * However, that being said, as one reputable American psychiatrist proves: "The concept of homosexuality as a permanent orientation is, however, without scientific validation; the notion is entirely politically grounded."(5) Due to vice-like grip of the Western liberal academic establishment on the media and education, it would surprise many to know how many non-genetic factors influence a person towards homosexuality (i.e. societal attitudes, peer pressure, loneliness, and having suffered sexual abuse as a child). The pioneering work of JONAH (Jews Offering New Alternatives to Homosexuality (6)) has been proven that a great, unknown percentage of cases can be treated. Such individuals can learn to completely alter their inner feelings, and come to live normal, healthy heterosexual lives. The stakes are not only spiritual: Again — due to today's political climate — the world public is not sufficiently informed about the medical dangers of homosexuality, which are greatly understated. (6) * * *

In a case of bestiality, which is defined as intercourse with mammals and birds, the animal is not to be put to death, as it would be in the case of the sin of an Israelite. *[Laws of Kings & Wars 9:8[6]])*

Adultery

Since there is no recognized rite or ceremony of marriage or divorce for Noahides; in order to understand the capital crime of adultery, *we must first understand when Noahide marriage begins and ends.*

Noahide Marriage: Noahides are considered married specifically from the time of a woman's first intercourse with her husband for the sake of marriage by mutual agreement, in either his or her place of residence. There is no officially prescribed ceremony. So long as it does not constitute idolatry and does not become recognized as an obligatory religious rite, any normative wedding ceremony is permitted.

Noahide Divorce: Besides death, Noahide marriage can end in divorce. However tragic and destructive it can be, divorce is fully permitted both to Noahides and Jews. The divorce is recognized by law from when the man expels his wife from his home, or when she leaves his premises on her own accord. *Actually, when either one actually takes action to leave or expel the other, they are divorced. (Laws of Kings & Wars 9:12[8], cf. Laws of Marriage 1:1 [found in 'Book of Women'])*

Should they later decide to rejoin and live together as man and wife; they are once again considered married.

- In a case of adultery of a non-Jewess by a non-Jew, vaginal (not anal) intercourse is specifically required for capital punishment. On the contrary, adultery of a Jewess by a non-Jew is punishable by death whether it was vaginal or anal, and even from the time she is betrothed to her husband, long before consummation. (7) *(Laws of Kings and Wars 9:10).* However, if a non-Jew had *consensual* relations (not a case of rape) with a single, unbetrothed Jewess above the age of majority the non-Jew is not liable for the death penalty. (8) *(Book of Holiness, Laws of Forbidden Sexual Relations 12:8[9])*

* * * *Although the non-Jew is technically not liable before an earthly court, a non-Jew who knowingly commits such an act can surely expect Divine retribution. Such consensual relations are a perverse and morally reprehensible act, being a desecration of the sanctity of a daughter of Israel, and thereby the Jewish People (the nation designated by HaShem as mankind's priesthood) as a whole. Besides the moral damage to society, a child born from such a union – although he is a Jew — is likely to suffer the most.* * * *

- In a case of adultery of a non-Jew with a *betrothed* Jewess; if convicted, the non-Jewish adulterer is to be tried according to the Laws of Israel. Before entering her husband's home, any adulterer — Jew or non-Jew — is liable to death by stoning. If the crime occurs after she has entered her husband's home, he is liable to death by strangulation. Only if the crime occurs after she has consummated her marriage, is the non-Jew tried according to the Noahide Laws, and he is liable to beheading by the sword. *(Ibid. 9:10[7])*

And just as the male adulterer is punished, so is his consenting female partner — the adulteress — liable for the death penalty, be she a Jewess or Noahidess.

Incest

For a Noahide, incest includes intercourse with one's mother, one's sister from the same mother, and any of his father's current or previous wives. Even if he was born of a fleeting, casual act intercourse; in regards to these laws, the one who bore him remains his mother, and the one by whom he was conceived, his father. *(Laws of Kings & Wars 9:7[5])* The prohibition of intercourse with a father's wife continues even after the father's death. *(Laws of Forbidden Sexual Relations 9:8[6])*

While other forms of sexual deviance — such as marital relations with one's daughter or paternal sister — are forbidden to Israelites by Torah Law, may be considered despicable, and could even be damaging to the individuals involved and society at large, they are not punishable by law for Noahides.

* * * *While the permissibility of these acts may seem revolting to us, it is assumed that mutual consent is involved. In the modern world, the reality of fathers consorting with their daughters is commonly heard of more in the context of cases of sexual abuse than in the context of mutual consent. Often times that abuse exists with other cruelties perpetrated by the father on his family. In such cases, because the father forces himself on his daughter, it becomes rape, an act of kidnapping, which is punishable by death.*

Even in the context of consensual relations; in our society, we may not easily understand the reasons for these permitted exceptions of what we may intuitively feel to be incest. However, the reasons exist:

> **Question 1:** Why the distinction between one's maternal sibling and one's paternal sibling?
>
> **Answer:** There is a principle in Torah, that HaShem has 'come down' to man's level, to give us Torah commandments that nearly all of us can keep, whatever our backgrounds, whatever our circumstances. Now although it may seem strange in the modern world, there is a sad reality known to the Almighty that in many non-Jewish

societies over the ages, many people did not know with certainty who their father is — much less who are their paternal siblings from differing mothers. However, in all societies, children nearly always grow up under their mothers' care, and know who their maternal siblings are. It is therefore rational that HaShem, in His mercy, not define father-daughter relations and relations with one's paternal sister as capital crimes deserving of death.

In contrast, with rare exception, this was not the case in Jewish societies throughout the ages. Furthermore, in the laws He gave to his chosen priestly nation, HaShem wanted to demonstrate the moral ideal. Fittingly, father-daughter intercourse (with testimony and warning) is a capital offense for Jews, while brother-sister relations are a severe crime as well, carrying the penalty of spiritual excision.

The important exception to this allowance is rape, which is a capital crime. Rape is listed here under the Noahide Commandment against stealing.

Question 2: *If that is so, that the Torah does not hold a man liable to what he cannot keep, then how could a non-Jew (who may not even know his father) be liable for lying with any of his father's current or previous wives, or any woman with whom he has had sexual relations even after his death?*

Answer: *The principle of HaShem's compassion still remains in tact: If one made a genuine mistake, having relations with a forbidden woman whom he believed to be permitted, he would be exempt from punishment.*

Now for various reasons, HaShem could not obligate the entire human race to honor their parents; hence there is no express legal Noahide obligation to do so. That is despite parental honor being a cornerstone Torah principle — one of the Ten Statements [a.k.a. "The Ten Commandments"] spoken at Mount Sinai. In fact, the Torah's special wording likens the honor of parents to the honor of HaShem Himself! It is in the moral bedrock prohibition of adultery that the principle of parental honor enters the Noahide Laws: in the case of a father's wife, it is an even wider, more sweeping Noahide prohibition with no "minimum amounts." A father's sexual partner is considered like his spouse whether she was his wife, his one time consort, or even rape victim, and even after his death.* * *

5
Stealing

This broad prohibition includes:

- **robbery** — stealing from someone openly

- **theft** — stealing in secret
    The above include even stealing an object of the slightest value. (To understand this principle, see Part I, *The Price of Freedom: Understanding the Inflexibility of the Noahide Laws*)

- **not returning borrowed property**

- **not returning a lost object whose owner has not given up on finding**

- **fraud** (such as using counterfeit currency as legal tender)
    Non-Jews are not liable in cases of doubt. Therefore one who uses currency that is more likely to be good than not; even if there is a significant chance it is

counterfeit, he cannot be held liable if indeed it is and he is caught. Likewise, if an owner has reason to believe an object is more likely than not to be his own; even if there is a significant chance it may be lost, he is not liable for not returning the object if indeed it *is* lost and it is found in his possession.

- **use of fraudulent weights or measures in business**

- **dishonest representation of any article for sale or rent by the owner or seller**

- **causing damage to property**, whether by direct or indirect means

- **unlawful trespassing the border of a neighbor's property**

- **not paying damages incurred in causing physical injury to someone else**

- **an employee making idle use of paid time**
  A worker is permitted to eat from what he is working with, such as eating grapes while harvesting them from the vines. *(Book of Judgments, Laws of Hiring 12:1)* The above prohibition includes eating on paid time during a task that does not involve food. However, rules of what a worker may and may not do on paid time are subject to the custom of the place, or his contract. If his contract (or local custom in absence of a contract) allows him to eat, then he is permitted. In our day and age, according to one's contract, chatting with and texting friends or playing computer games on paid time may be more common examples of criminal idleness by workers.

  However, non-Jews are not liable for accidental transgressions. For example, an employee who was idle because he was misled as to the actual time of day, one who damaged property due to forces beyond his control, and one who unknowingly trespassed a neighbor's border, are clearly exempt. However, if the individual was aware of the facts, ignorance of the law is not an excuse: the willing transgressor who was aware of his actions is liable.

- **withholding wages from a worker** *(Book of Judgments, Laws of Hiring 11:1-2)*

- **not paying debts or fulfilling financial obligations of lawful contracts on time**
  Noahides are not liable for failure to fulfill financial obligations (i.e. paying damages, wages, debts, etc.) due to genuine lack of funds. There is no punishment in Torah law for being impoverished – no debtor's prison or indentured servitude, as exists in Torah Law for Jews in certain circumstances who are unable to pay what they owe. Only one who clearly *had* the means yet *still* didn't pay is liable. Noahide societies may enact just civil laws to prevent abuse of this humane system.

- **not paying just taxes in accordance with the laws of one's country of residence**
  Justly administered taxes, such as those that pay for utilities and public roads shared by all, can be essential to the functioning of an urban society. The legality of others, such as income tax, is not as simple. On the contrary: according to the Noahide Laws, in a case of a tax that constitutes thievery of the public, it is not the citizens who are liable but the government.

- **other definitions of theft, depending on the laws of one's country of residence**
  Theft of intellectual property is an example. Another example is slander with the intent the cause monetary damage. However, for an action forbidden by government legislation to constitute the capital Noahide offense of theft; *it must conform to the basic definition from the Torah - that ownable property was physically taken from or withheld from its rightful owner.* Otherwise, although it may be penal in one's local system of civil law, it does not constitute a violation of Noahide Law.

* * * *Here lies the rabbinical principle of "the law of the kingdom is the law." Enjoying autonomy under the benign rulership of Babylonia, the Talmudic sages recognized the above rule in the context of a society's property and financial laws. (For more on righteous government Section B-4g)* * * *

- **kidnapping**

- **rape**
  Rape is a form of kidnap, which is a type of theft of a human being. It is therefore a capital crime according to the Seven Laws. (Laws of Kings & Wars 9:13[9]) The classical example of this is the rape of Dinah, who was an unmarried Noahidess (the Hebrews only received the legal status of Israelites when they accepted the entire Torah at Mount Sinai). Note that "thou shall not steal" in the "Ten Commandments" (part of Israel's Torah) specifically refers to the theft of a person, which is a capital crime for Jews as well. *(Exodus 20:12, Deut. 5:16 cf. Book of Injuries, Laws of Theft 9:1)*

Please note, the laws of stealing are intricate. They require proper study to avoid transgression.

6
Eating Meat Removed From A Living Animal

Not to eat raw flesh or cooked meat removed from an animal before it has completely ceased to convulse after slaughter or death by other means, be it a domesticated or non-domesticated mammal, from the pure species (that can be offered on the altar) or impure species (that cannot be offered). Again: the capital prohibition for non-Jews does not apply to bird flesh and certainly not fish. It only applies to *mammals*, both kosher and non-kosher species. *(Laws of Kings & Wars 9:15-16[11-13])*

* * * According to the Oral tradition, the above is the true meaning of the HaShem's Command to Noah, "however flesh with its lifeblood you shall not consume" (Gen. 9:4 cf. Book of Holiness, Laws of Forbidden Foods 5:1). There was never a Divine prohibition against consuming blood that was removed from a non-living animal for non-Jews; only for Israel. Despite the overly literal reading, blood — even from a living creature — is not forbidden for Noahide consumption. (Laws of Kings & Wars 14-17[10-14]) * * *

For an explanation of what store-bought meat may be consumed, see Part IV, Question #18.

7
Establishing Justice: Enforcing The Law

A sane non-Jewish adult (above the age of puberty) who, under his own free will (not under coercion), intentionally (not accidentally) transgresses any one of the Noahide Laws, *is liable to beheading by the sword.* This is the obligation to establish a system of judges in every city to judge according to the Noahide laws and enforce them accordingly, and to warn the public against transgressing them. *(Laws of Kings & Wars 9:17[14] cf. 10:3[2])*

Cases may be judged and punishment ordained even by a single male judge, and based on the testimony of a single person — even a family member, but not the testimony of a woman. *(Ibid. 9:19[14])*

* * * *This may seem to the modern mind as an example of the inequality of men and women in Torah law. In truth, however, there are a number of important reasons for this, none of which are sexist. The same Torah by which these laws were ordained, contains the accounts in Genesis of the superior judgment of Sarah and Rebecca to that of their husbands. It is by the same Bible in which Deborah ruled as a Judge over all Israel, the leader of her generation, and one of the seven great prophetesses of Israelite history. Nevertheless, in the same Torah from Heaven, we learn of the counsel of Jethro regarding the appointment of judges in Israel, and how Moses implemented HaShem's Commandment to do so: It is not enough that judges be wise: they must also be privately wealthy and warriors. That is to strengthen them against attempts by litigants to bribe, blackmail, and threaten them. Indeed there is at least one notable example of a female warrior in Israelite history: Deborah the Judge. However, it is Divine wisdom that a woman — naturally the foundation of* her home, nurturer and anchor of her children and grandchildren — not be subjected to the dangers and threats faced by judges. * * *

An entire city can be judged guilty and liable for capital punishment for not bringing their criminals to justice. The classical example of this is the city of Shechem. The prince of the chieftain Hamor kidnapped and raped Jacob's daughter Dinah. Although the citizens of the Shechem were witnesses and well aware of what the prince had done, they did nothing to put him to justice. Fittingly, they were all, except for the women and children, liable. *(Ibid. 9:19[14])* (For a deeper analysis of Simeon and Levi's execution of Noahide justice, see Part III, *Refraining from Cruel Anger.)*

There are many cases in which non-Jews who violate the Noahide Laws are exempt from any punishment, such as situations of doubt, accidental transgression, coercion, and more.

For example, if a non-Jew who violated the Noahide Laws under threat to his life (not merely for fear of a lesser penalty or danger), he is completely exempt from punishment. A non-Jew is under no obligation to sanctify the Name of Heaven, to give up his own life rather than transgress. Even if he committed idolatry or murder under threat of his life, he is exempt. *However, ignorance of the law is not an acceptable excuse,* and does not exempt a transgressor from punishment.

One technical exception is adultery of a non-Jew with a *betrothed* Jewess (who is still unmarried). As explained in above in Law #4. In this case, if convicted, the non-Jewish adulterer is tried according to the Laws of Israel. Before entering her husband's home, any adulterer — Jew or non-Jew — is liable to death by stoning. If the crime occurs after she has entered her husband's home, he is liable to death by strangulation. Only if the crime occurs after she has consummated her marriage, is the non-Jew tried according to the Noahide Laws, and he is liable to beheading by the sword. *(Ibid. 9:10[7])*

And just as the male adulterer is punished, so is his consenting female partner — the adulteress — liable for the death penalty, be she a Jewess or Noahidess.

For a full list of exemptions for violations of the Noahide Laws, see Section C: *Cases for Exemption from the Noahide Laws.*

* * * The Noahide Laws are considered so basic that they can be arrived at through common logic. (Laws of Kings & Wars 9:2[1]) Furthermore, they are the bedrock moral foundation by which a just, Godly society can exist. If ignorance were an acceptable excuse, the laws would be undermined so easily that they would be impossible to implement on a wide scale.

As explained above (Part I, Noahide Justice in Perspective) it may seem "unfair" at first that Jews are not equally liable for the death penalty as non-Jews according to the Seven Laws. For example, a Jew is not liable for the death penalty for stealing or for cursing the Creator with any other appellation for HaShem — only with one of the seven holy Names of HaShem. In truth, however, Jews have many more Commandments which carry punishments that are more varied and severe. Besides beheading, there is also death by stoning, strangulation, and burning. Again, except for emergency cases, there is no capital punishment in Israel — not for Jews or Noahides — before the renewal of the Sanhedrin and its restoration to the Chamber of the Hewn Stone in a rebuilt Temple. (Book of Judges, Laws of Sanhedrin 14:11[10]) * * *

B
Laws Not Included In
The Seven Commandments

* * * *Unlike the Seven Noahide Laws of Section A, willful violation of these rabbinical precepts does not remove a Noahide from the Life of the World to Come, the eternal reward for the righteous after this life. Nevertheless, it is a criminal act for which he can expect Divine punishment if he does not repent.* * * *

1. THE PROHIBITIONS

a. **Honoring the sanctity of the Holy Temple**

- *Not entering the precise borders of the outer courtyard (hheyl) around the Holy Temple.* Beyond that border, only sanctified, born-Jews, Levites, and *kohen*-priests are permitted to enter. *(Book of Service, Laws of the Chosen House 7:16, Laws of Entry into the Sanctuary 3:5)* Although the Temple no longer stands, its sanctity remains forever. Therefore, this affects where a non-Jew may go if he visits the Temple Mount today. *Although it is not enforced today, this is the only prohibition for non-Jews outside the Seven Laws that is a capital offense.*

    This is a Jewish law that is not enforced by Noahide courts, but the *kohen*-priests on duty; nevertheless, it translates into a prohibition for the non-Israelite.

    This has nothing to do with anyone being superior or more worthy; it has to do with the roles assigned by the Creator to different groups of people. Similarly, regular Israelites could not venture into the sacred areas permitted only to Levites and *kohen*-priests.

Just as the *kohanim* are Israel's priests, Israel is to be a kingdom of priests to the nations. This truth is reflected in the sacred zoning of Holy Temple.

- Not to give any Temple offering, except the `olah – a whole-burnt offering. This may be a bull, male sheep, male goat, or pigeon be it male or female *(ibid. Laws of Sacrificial Procedures 1:8)*; as long as the animal is found to be kosher, even the `olah offering of an idolater will be offered by the *kohen*-priests. This is a Jewish law that is not enforced by Noahide courts, but the *kohen*-priests on duty; nevertheless, it translates into a prohibition for the non-Israelite. *(Ibid. 3:1)*

b. **A non-Jewess is not to have consensual sexual intercourse with a Jew.** A non-Jewess who has consensual relations with a Jew (she was not raped) is considered to be a stumbling block, and liable to be put to death. *(Book of Holiness, Forbidden Sexual Relations 12:8[9]).* As difficult as this might be for many in the modern world to accept; for the learned Bible believer, this is known not to be a petty xenophobic ruling of human commands. This law is explicitly stated in the Torah of Moses. *(Numbers 31:16-17) And the Jew is not absolved of responsibility for his crime: he is liable to lashes by the whip for defiance of rabbinical law.*

c. **Not to strike an Israelite out of evil intent, causing even the least bit of physical damage.**

* * * *This law is analogous to the capital Torah offense for Israelites of cursing and striking parents (Exodus 21:15,17 — yet another example of the greater severity of certain commandments incumbent upon Israel that are not incumbent upon the world. (see Part I, Noahide Justice in Perspective) and the grave sin of disgracing Torah teachers. (Book of Knowledge, Laws of Repentance 3:25[14])*

Rather than an example of unfairness towards non-Jews, this Law preserves the proper place of Israel — HaShem's chosen nation of priests — among the nations. (Exodus 19:6) It is also a token of HaShem's justice towards Israel: From the onset days of Abraham, the Hebrews have always faced enemies in greater numbers and in positions of power. Against such odds, this law serves as an extra measure of justice for the nation with a most dangerous and largely thankless mission in a ruthless world.) * * *

d. **Forbidden idolatrous customs** *(minhagoth 'avodah zarah) (Book of Kings 9:4):*

- Not to erect a "pillar" (*maSevah*). This is an large stone or a mound of stones that was erected as a center for the public to gather for idol worship. This even includes a pillar erected for the service of HaShem, as the Hebrew patriarch Jacob did. *(Laws of Kings and Wars 9:4[2] cf. Laws of Idolatry 6:9[6])*

* * * *It may seem ironic that Noahides are forbidden here to imitate the pious action of Jacob, the righteous founding father of the Jewish People. However, the Sages understood that even pillars erected in righteous piety often became centers of idol worship in the future. Verily, Beth El — the site Jacob consecrated to be the site of a future Temple to HaShem — became one of the two national centers of silver calf worship of the Northern Ten tribes, the kingdom of Israel. (I Kings 12:26-33)* * * *

- Not to plant an *asherah*-tree. This is a tree planted near a place of idol worship, for the public to come and gather there. *(Laws of Idolatry 6:14[9])* It is forbidden to plant such a tree even next to an altar for sacrifice to *HaShem*.

* * * *Noahides are permitted to build such an altar in almost any place in our times. The law is stricter for Jews, who are* *only permitted to sacrifice on the precise place of the holy altar on the Temple Mount, Mount Moriah.* * * *

- Not to make a statue or carved figure (specifically convex, not concave) of the human figure, even for beauty. This is so that others not be led astray, thinking they are for idolatry. *(Ibid. 3:15-16[10])*

- Other customs with idolatrous roots, such as candles on a birthday cake, the custom of a bride giving her bridegroom a wedding ring, the Christian position of prayer (on bent knees with hands clasped), etc. — while forbidden to Jews — are not forbidden to Noahides.

e. **Not to cross-breed animal species.** To our understanding, non-Jews are not technically liable for modern genetic engineering that involves splicing genes from one creature into the genome of another. Only one who actually cross-breeds distinct species of creatures in order to produce vital offspring is liable. Although this contradicts the scientific definition of a distinct species (one that that cannot produce vital offspring when mated to another), it is recorded in the Oral legends that this activity was widespread before the Flood of Noah. There may well have been a process known to the ancients that is not presently understood. One modern example of this prohibition is the cross-breeding of a horse with a donkey to produce a mule.

f. **Not to graft trees belonging to Jews.** *(Book of Seeds, Laws of Diverse Varieties 1:4[6])* Although the law does not actually forbid a Noahide from grafting different species of his own trees together; despite the breakthroughs of modern genetic engineering (i.e. the "brocco-flower" and other hybrids), we cannot know how dangerous this activity may prove to be in the long term, as pure species with unique properties are altered forever.

g. **For non-Jews to be occupied in the study of the entire Torah, like a Jew, but only in the realm of the Noahide Laws (and responsibilities of the nations).** It is not clear that this applies to Noahides; we therefore interpret this law to apply specifically to non-Noahide gentiles. Since they do not even uphold the Seven Laws, it is inappropriate for them to study more than the sections of the portions of the Hebrew Bible that pertain to Noahide faith, their law and its application (such as the Torah book of Genesis, and the books of Jonah and Job), as well as the Oral Law pertaining specifically to the Seven Laws. That actually leaves much of *Mishneh Torah* available to them to read, since many sections of law are included in the realm of Noahide Law.

To our understanding, the only Torah that is clearly forbidden to a Noahide is the un-restated Oral Law: the raw primary works of the early Sages such as *Mishnah*, the classical works of *halakhic* expositions (*Sifre*, *Mekhilta*, etc.), and the two Talmuds. If such is the case regarding early practical legal sources, how much more so works of the *kabbalah* (esoteric mystical wisdom) such as the *Zohar*.

* * * **WHAT TO STAY AWAY FROM:** *While Kabbalistic literature contains deep and great wisdom, it is poorly understood even by trained Torah scholars. The most famous work, the Zohar, mentions and prescribes ancient practices and promotes opinions that remained outside of, and even contradict the halakhah (applied Torah law) as it was codified. It includes allegorical descriptions of concepts that, if taken literally, contradict foundational tenets of the Oral tradition. This is especially true of Sefer Yetzirah and Sefer ha-Bahir. Finally, Zohar is a layered work, with text that was, with no doubt, added later.*

Written in terse style with highly symbolic language, Zohar requires (1) Fluency in Aramaic (not to mention Hebrew); (2) Very strong grounding in the halakhah (law) and the nuances of the language of the Sages; (3) A broad and critical mind; (4) The guidance of an expert teacher who does not consider Zohar a source of practical halakhah, who can identify a portion of text that was added later, and can explain the allegorical meaning of passages that appear to contradict the Oral tradition. (Few such teachers remain.)

While it is more organized and deeply profound, un-grounded scholars are similarly confused by Lurianic kabbalah. If trained Jewish scholars stumble in the study of mystical kabbalah, how much less fitting is it for Noahides.

WHAT MAY BE STUDIED: *To my understanding, Noahides who yearn for a greater spiritual closeness to the Creator should focus first on mastering the first book of Mishneh Torah, the Book of Knowledge, where he can gain the most accurate, simple understanding of the foundations of proper Torah belief and practice.*

Once a student is firmly rooted in the proper belief in the Oneness of HaShem (as described in Part II Law #1 and Appendix II) and that our respective Covenants with HaShem are based on our fulfilling the Laws He gave us, the Noahide student may venture into mainstream Torah literature that can help him refine his character. In the absence of a detailed, practical guide in Mishneh Torah as to how to achieve the character requirements defined in Laws of Personal Dispositions, one such guide I recommend is "The Trail to Tranquility" by Rabbi Lazer Brody. (© Emunah Outreach Publications, 2008) Written by a master, veteran counselor, it is a simple yet effective, practical guide to ridding one's life of the most destructive character flaws – anger and arrogance – and achieving joy through simple faith in HaShem.

Again, firmly rooted in the laws and outlook of Mishneh Torah, one may read "Hishtap'hhuth ha-Nefesh" – Outpouring of the Soul. Written by arguably the greatest of the Hassidic masters, Rebbe Nahhman of Breslov, this short practical guidebook to prayer and meditation is clearly rooted in the ancient path of the prophets.

A much larger and more difficult guidebook to the awesome ways of prophets is 'Sefer ha-Maspiq le`Ovde-HaShem' (The Guide to Serving God) by the RaMBaM's son, Rav Avraham ha-hhasid.

Rather than offering a glimpse into that which was meant to remain hidden, these works focus on what a person can do to intensify his spiritual experience of closeness to the Almighty.
* * *

Most importantly, the entire Hebrew Bible and Mishneh Torah are open for Noahides to study. Fittingly, if a Noahide genuinely wishes to fulfill a specific commandment *outside* of the Noahide Laws and seeks instruction in doing so properly — he may learn either from a live or written source.

The key points of this Law for non-Noahide gentiles are:

- **Not to study all the Commandments as a whole for their own sake** — *as a Jew is obligated to do.* One reason for this is that anything less than a comprehensive, accurate study of the width and breadth of Torah (Oral Law) over many years, under the guidance of a master, is certain to yield misunderstandings, misapplication of the law, confusion and error. And that is assuming pure intentions on the part of the reader... More often, this kind of Torah study by non-believers is secular poison that, under the guise of pure academia, deconstructs the text according to the culture-bound, liberal mindset of Western intellectuals — even relegating Torah to the realm of mythology.

- **Not to study unrelated Torah literature out of curiosity or as a leisurely or academic pursuit.** Rather one is to concentrate purely on his/her obligations and voluntarily accepted Commandments alone.

* * * *Consider what history has taught us about the damage of unrestricted Torah study by the nations. Until the lifetime of Abraham (when they were all but forgotten), the ways of HaShem were known orally. It was only to Israel that a written Torah was given. And HaShem had the august judicial body — the Sanhedrin — appointed to interpret and teach its laws to the nation and to the world. Ideally, a member of the Nations seeking to learn the will of the One, True Creator would come to the Jewish sages for guidance; just as Jacob studied under the guidance of Shem and Ever (Sefer Ha-Yashar parashath Toledoth). They would teach him what he must know in order to serve the Creator as his fathers of old: Noah, Shem, Ham and Japheth.*

Sadly, the system collapsed. Israel was thrust into exile with no king, no active priesthood or Sanhedrin — yet the words of the written Torah became widely known. The result of Torah in the hands of idolaters without the guidance of its proper teachers has been 2,000 years of disaster. A world full of peoples and creeds warring with one another over contradicting views on Torah, its commandments, and the ultimate Messiah-king. History is proof that the unguided study of the entire Written and Oral Law — particularly by idolaters — has led to confusion, heretical ideas, rampant sin, and persecution of the Jews. * * *

h. **Not to invent a new religion, create new religious rites, or add other religious obligations to be regarded as obligatory.**

Noahides may not create their own original customs of worship, religious ceremonies, or any other religious obligations to be treated as law or set in stone. Even preaching that a non-Jew must be circumcised in order to inherit the Life of the World to Come, transgresses this prohibition. *A non-Jew must either become full a convert to Torah Judaism, taking upon himself all the Commandments, or remain under the Noahide Covenant, neither adding nor diminishing from it. (Book of Judges, Laws of Kings & Wars 10:12[9])*

For example, while a community or an individual is free to develop its own prayer ceremony, they may not relate to it as having the force of law. Since HaShem left matters of worship and ceremony as a matter of personal choice for Noahides, it should remain that way.

Nonetheless, *a Noahide is fully permitted to perform any of the other Commandments given to Israel – Torah obligations and rabbinical ordinances – on a volunteer basis.* This even includes wrapping *tefillin* and placing *mezuzoth* on doorposts. *(See Section B)*

Exceptions to this include unlimited Torah study, the *halakhic* observance of Sabbath and the Jewish festivals, giving any other Temple offering besides the `olah (a whole-burnt offering), and making a pilgrimage to the Temple as a Jew, which entails entering the Temple's outer courtyard *(hheyl)*.

This law contradicts those who would condone Islam or other monotheistic religions as Noahide. To create a new religion was forbidden to them from the start. The only *dath* (religious law) – is the Torah, both for Jews and non-Jews, according to their respective Covenants.

However, as mentioned above, a Noahide who, in violation of this precept, is a member of a Christian church or Muslim mosque or adds religious obligations – although he is worthy of punishment – still has a place in the World to Come.

i. Not to observe a day of complete cessation from all manner of labor like the Jewish Sabbath, even on another day of the week, neither to observe a festival in the manner of Jews – be it Jewish or original. *(Ibid. 10:11[9])*

Unlike other religious obligations, a Noahide may not elect to observe a full *halakhic* Sabbath or Festival rest as a Jew even on a volunteer basis.

Noahides may indeed observe a general day of rest: a day of leisure, togetherness and Torah study with family, friends and community. They may enjoy a day off from work on which they can connect to God spiritually. But they must not do so like Jews, who must cease from all activities defined by the Torah as "labor" in regards to the Sabbath. They must enjoy their day off in a manner that involves some type of creative activity that constitutes a Torah prohibition to the Jew on that day. Rabbinical Sabbath prohibitions for Jews – such as playing music or handling money – are not enough; neither are activities that break the "spirit of Shabbat" for Jews, such as watching television.

For example, a Noahide might enjoy a simple family outing with a car on his day of rest. This involves kindling a flame, since fire is repeatedly ignited and extinguished in the car engine. It also involves carrying objects in the public domain. Even a short, refreshing walk with a bottle of water is sufficient.

However, carrying and transferring flame are permitted to Jews on a festival. Therefore, on Jewish festivals, Noahides may celebrate, but in a way that generates forbidden "labors" for the Jew. Examples include kindling a fire in the fireplace or a camp-fire to gather around for Torah study, taking the time to hand-write poetry or create artwork on the theme of the festival. These are enjoyable activities that provide leisure and remembrance of the festival, yet ensure that the legal observance of Sabbath and Festival remain the sole inheritance of the nation of Israel. This honors HaShem's original plan for the world. *(See below)*

* * * Like other Noahide Laws that can be interpreted in a negative light, this law is no slight or insult to the non-Jew, God-forbid. Rather, it is a reflection of the distinct roles within humanity that HaShem desired in His world. We see this in the blessing the Noah's blessing to his sons (Gen. 9:26-27), and later on in the blessings Isaac prepared for, and gave both his sons, Esau and Jacob. (Ibid. ch.27) Both Shem and Jacob (Gen. 28:1-4: Jacob was Shem's direct descendant and his student in Shem's final years), both progenitors of Israel in their own right were charged by their prophet-fathers with a distinct priestly role. Similarly, Japheth and Esau were blessed with success in the development of the material world. (Note the blessing Isaac had reserved for Esau, and how Esau was indeed blessed.) This role – to "conquer" and develop the physical world – is a key part of the original task given to Adam from his creation. (Gen. 1:28)

Amazingly, if one considers the main contributions of the peoples descended from Shem and Jacob vis a vis those derived from Japheth and Esau through history, one can readily discern this general pattern. * * *

2. The Obligation of Circumcision For Arabic Peoples

Offspring of Abraham with Keturah are obligated to perform circumcision on the eighth day of a male child's life. This includes all Arabic peoples, since the descendents of Ishmael and Abraham through Keturah have thoroughly intermingled. *(Laws of Kings and Wars 10:10[8])*

It is interesting that this law was legislated despite the rabbinical rule that the nations of the world have been thoroughly mixed by the Assyrian warlord Sennacherib, thereby eliminating the biblical categories of "Edomite", "Egyptian", "Amalekite", etc. It is possible that the rabbis viewed the Arabian Peninsula to be an exception (It was, after all, centuries before the Arabs — inspired by their new religion of Islam — expanded mightily beyond their traditional homeland). However, it is clear from various sources that the Torah views the foreskin as an abomination, and circumcision an ideal rectification that should be spread to humanity. It is possible that since Arabic peoples already practiced circumcision, it would be easy to spread this rectification among them.

In our times, Arabic peoples are even more mixed, with Persian, Greek, Jewish, Crusader and African blood, etc. *Only descendants of the few families with a clear, undisputed patrilineal tradition from the pre-Muslim-era might consider this a legal injunction. There is no legal obligation for Noahides to fulfill their commandments in a case of genuine doubt.* However, on a purely moral level (considering how repulsive the foreskin is in eyes of Torah, and how lofty the deed of circumcision *[Book of Love, Laws of Circumcision 3:8-9])* and for the sake of health, all Arabic peoples and non-Jews in general would be wise to embrace circumcision.

3. The Gift of Repentance and the 'Life of the World To Come'

The opportunity to repent for one's sins before *HaShem* and to be forgiven — regardless of whether or not one was convicted — is a precious gift shared by Jews and Noahides. *HaShem*, in His Compassion, gave mankind the means to know the behavior that He desires, and that He hates. This gives us the ability to be clean before Him in our physical lives, and to inherit the eternal afterlife, the 'life of the World to Come.' *(Book of Knowledge, Laws of Repentance 3:26[14] cf. Book of Judges, Laws of Kings and Wars 8:14[11])*

Even if one faces certain death for one's sins, or has reached his deathbed after a lifetime of sin, he can still repent: That repentance can still save him from the utter destruction of the soul, and earn Him that blissful eternity of basking in radiance of the Divine Presence.

The laws of Repentance, found in the Book of Knowledge are many, and deserve careful study. However, in short:

- **For sins between man and *HaShem*** (i.e. eating flesh removed from a living animal, forbidden consensual sexual intercourse, etc.), one performs the following <u>spoken</u> confession. *(Laws of Repentance 1:2)* Silently thinking these thoughts in the heart is not enough.

    a. *"HaShem, I have sinned, I have knowingly transgressed, and I have willfully disobeyed before You.*
    b. *"I have done such and such...* (he then proceeds to confess his sinful actions in detail)
    c. *"and behold, I regret and am ashamed of my deeds...* (Here he feels remorse for the sin. If one is moved to tears, this is the remorse that is proper.)
    d. *"and I will never repeat this sin again."* (Here one accepts upon oneself never repeat this action again with full intent.)

The very definition of repentance is that the sinner abandons his sin and removes it from his very thought-process, and resolves in his heart never to do it again. If he merely goes through the procedure without truly making this resolution in his heart, his repentance is invalid. One knows he has truly repented when he finds himself in the same situation with the full capacity to sin again, yet he refrains. *(Ibid. 2:1,3)*

* * * *A severe crime can be such that repentance alone does not guarantee HaShem's forgiveness. Rather, according to the severity of the crime, the person may experience suffering in his life — even death by the Hand of Heaven. However, if one has repented sincerely, these travails serve to complete his atonement, and he will merit the eternal reward of the righteous after this life — the "life of the World to Come." For the person who has turned his life around, living a life of repentance; personal sufferings in this world can be perceived as bittersweet gifts (since, through a finite amount of suffering in this world, he avoids the infinite punishment of losing his life of the World to Come). (7)* * * *

- **For sins between man and his fellow** (such as theft), the above confession is useless until forgiveness has been obtained from the offended party. It is not enough that he makes restitution (as in the case of theft); he must appease the person until forgiveness is obtained.

If the offended party refuses to forgive, the one seeking forgiveness sends a delegation of three friends who confront him and request him to relent. If he is still not appeased, a second and even a third delegation must be sent. However, if the offended party still refuses to forgive after that point, the penitent leaves him be. While he is now considered to have done enough, it is the obstinate 'offended party' that is now the sinner. *(Ibid. 2:11-13[9])*

Clearly, there are sins between man and his fellow for which one simply cannot repent and be absolved. For example, if one has stolen from an unknown number of people (i.e. cheating an unknown body of investors in the stock market), how can one reach every offended party and obtain forgiveness? One must be careful.

4. Rights of Non-Jews in Torah Law

Despite our differences in Torah obligations and legal status, the basic equality of all righteous human beings before *HaShem* is a fundamental concept in Torah Law. *(Book of Judges, Laws of Sanhedrin 12:7-8)* Moreover, we see in various laws in the below section that *HaShem*'s compassion often extends beyond the righteous even to include idolaters. *(Psalms 145:9 cf. Laws of Kings & Wars 10:16[12])*

The following laws were not codified as "rights of non-Jews" in the sources of the Oral Law. Nevertheless I have translated them as such for better comprehension by the modern reader, and to emphasize a point that cannot be overstated in our times. *Even in an ideal, fully-functioning Israelite society in which idolatry is not tolerated in the least; non-Jews are treated as human beings.*

a. **The right of Noahides to voluntarily observe any of the other Torah-commandments to which only Israelites are obligated** (for the sake of eternal reward).

As noted above, the only significant exceptions to this rule are the unlimited study of Torah, observing a full Sabbath or Festival rest like Jews, and the restrictions on Temple offerings and movement in the Temple precincts of non-Jews. Beyond these restrictions, regular non-Noahide gentiles are forbidden even to learn Torah that is outside the realm of the Seven Laws.

* * * *The logic is as follows. Once one has accepted upon himself the bedrock laws of humanity, he can then climb higher to fulfill other Torah precepts properly.* * * *

Tzitzith (Fringes), *Tefillin*, *Mezuzoth*

In regards to commandments such as wearing a *tallith* –a four-cornered garment with *tzitzith*-fringes by which one could be mistaken for a Jew — it is logical that wise Noahides (who understand the global importance of Jews keeping their laws properly) fulfill such commandments in a way that does not present a stumbling block for Jews. The same applies to wearing *tefillin* (phylacteries). Otherwise, a righteous, *tallith*-clad, *tefillin*-wrapped Noahide driving a car on the Sabbath day could appear as a Jewish transgressor, creating a scandal. For a similar reason, it is forbidden to Jews to sell a fringed *tallith* to a non-Noahide gentile. *(Book of Love, Laws of Tzitzit 3:9)*

The Commandment of *mezuzah* (only obligatory for Jews) is to affix a special, tanned leather parchment with handwritten passages from the Torah in a protective case to the doorposts of one's home. Out of concern that this could cause Noahides to be mistaken for Jews, one who wishes to voluntarily fulfill this precept is commonly instructed to affix the *mezuzah* of his main entrance to the *inside* of the doorpost, so that it will not be visible from the outside. However, this does not fulfill the Commandment of *mezuzah*, and the Noahide has every right to fulfill this precept according to law, earning him eternal reward. Notably, the Talmudic Sages made no objection to this.

I therefore recommend that Noahides who volunteer to fulfill the precept of *mezuzah* do so according to law without fear, but place a visible, attractive placard just below it stating:

"In voluntary fulfillment of God's Commandment to Israel, this *mezuzah* graces a Noahide home, not a Jewish home."

This allows the Noahide to receive eternal reward for fulfilling the precept properly, while preventing misunderstanding.

b. **The right of non-Jews to be judged according to the Laws of Israel, if both parties so request.**

However, if one party does not so desire, he is not forced. There is no obligation to be judged by any legal system other than the Seven Commandments. *(Laws of Kings & Wars 10:15[12])*

c. **Protection from murder, rape and theft even by Jews** *(prohibitions on Jews that I am translating as the rights of non-Jews)*:

- Even outright idolaters that are not at war with Israel are protected by law from being killed in cold blood.

- Just as it is forbidden for Jews to lie with non-Jewesses, so are the latter protected by law from rape. If a Jew commits such a crime even in private (but with proper testimony, etc), he is liable to lashes of the whip by the court for defiance. If he does so in public, he is liable even to be killed by zealots on the spot with no trial. *(Book of Holiness, Laws of Forbidden Sexual Relations 12:4-7)*

- It is also forbidden for Jews to steal anything — even of the slightest value — from any human being, Jew or non-Jew. *(Book of Injuries, Laws of Theft 1:1)* This includes causing him to make a miscalculation. Rather Jews must be exacting in their business transactions even with an idolater. *(Ibid. 7:10[8])* Moreover, an idolater's property is to be protected from thieves just as that of a Jew. *(Ibid. Laws of Injury to Property 11:4[3])*

d. **The right to receive medical care:** Once the Jubilee year is in force, resident Noahides living in the Land of Israel will be eligible for the status of *gere-toshav* (resident aliens), giving them – among other privileges – the right to free medical treatment by Jews. This can occur when the Sanhedrin is restored. Until then, Noahides are entitled to Jewish medical care for a fee, and in certain cases even idolaters. *(Laws of Idolatry 10:1,3.)*

* * * *After the State of Israel's famous responses to the Indonesian tsunami of 2004 and Haiti disaster – particularly the incredible work of ZAKA, the Torah-observant team of Israeli paramedics – it should be clear to all how valiantly Torah-observant Jews respond even to idolaters in desperate need of help.)* * * *

e. **The right to honesty, basic kindness and humane treatment from Jews** (Duties of Jews that I am translating as the rights of non-Jews).

Jews must be honest and forthright with non-Jews as much as Jews. **It is plainly forbidden for Jews to deceive anyone, Jew or non-Jew, Noahide or idolater**, even outside of business. *(Book of Knowledge, Laws of Character Traits 2:11[6])* Similarly the sages rule that the Torah commandment that Jews rise before the aged *(Leviticus 19:32)* includes the non-Jewish elderly as the Jewish elderly: Jews must stand up before, honor with words, and give a supporting hand to any person of greatly advanced age *(Book of Knowledge, Laws of Torah Study 6:10[9])*. They also ruled that the non-Jewish sick be visited by Jews as the Jewish sick, that their dead be humanely buried by Jews as the Jewish dead, and that their poor be fed among the poor of Israel. *(Laws of Kings & Wars 10:16[12])*

This basic kindness even extends to the ruling that Jews should greet idolaters and ask of their welfare. Although there are certain limitations, this even applies on their idolatrous holiday. *(Book of Knowledge, Laws of Idolatry 10:8[5])*

f. **The limited rights to buy real property from Jews and dwell in the Land of Israel.** *(Laws of Idolatry 10:4-5[3-4])*

As *gere-toshav* – (resident aliens, whose laws are not discussed in this work) – Noahides will one day be permitted to freely reside in the Land of Israel. As explained above, this status will only exist in a time when the laws of the Jubilee are in force, which can happen once the Sanhedrin is restored. This special status entitles Noahides to free medical care. *(For more see "Regarding 'Geruth toshav' and Noahide Oaths.")*

Until that time, Jews are allowed to rent out buildings as storehouses (not for the purpose of residence) to both Noahides and idolaters, so long as they do not form a cluster of three or more structures together. This restriction does not apply outside of Israel, where Jews are entitled to sell homes and fields freely to non-Jews.

* * * *This is not a prohibition on the non-Jew to visit the land of Israel of his own volition; even for a lengthened period of time. Moreover, there is no prohibition on the non-Jew to seek out a place to rent in Israel; only for the Jew to rent it out. To our understanding, even if a Jew mistakenly does so, he has only unwittingly transgressed a rabbinical decree.*

To understand the reasoning behind these challenging laws, consider the corrupting influence of assimilated Jews in Israel throughout history — with their idolatry and Hellenist values. Imagine how much more intense that assimilating influence would be were there no laws limiting the dwelling of non-Jews in the Land. In fact, in enacting these protective decrees, the sages of the Sanhedrin were using the powers vested in them by the Torah itself (Deut. 17:8-13), to define the parameters of a Divine commandment: "They shall not dwell in your land, lest they cause you to sin against me." (Exodus 23:34) * * *

The land of Syria has partial sanctity, it being part of the "Greater Israel" promised to Abraham, but not the actual heartland promised to Moses. Fittingly, while it is permitted for Jews to sell homes freely to non-Jews (including Noahides) in Syria, it is forbidden to sell them fields, so as not to release the land of Israel from the obligation of tithes.

These real property laws apply thus so long as Israel is weak among the nations. Once Israel rises in power sufficiently; only non-Jews who have accepted upon themselves the Noahide Laws will be entitled to so much as pass through the Land of Israel. *This proves just how vitally essential is the practice of the Noahide Laws in eyes of HaShem.*

g. **The unwritten right to establish a righteous government**: *(The existence of this 'right' per se and the specific details are point of disagreement among scholars. The following explanation follows the understanding of the author.)*

The Sages respected the basic, unwritten right of non-Jews to voluntarily elect a righteous government, even one that imposes a fair system of taxes and monetary laws for the preservation of the society. The Sages expressed this right in the words *dinah de-malkhutha dinah*, meaning *"the law of the land is law."* That statement was specifically in the context of the *monetary laws* of an upright government like that of Babylonia in their time: one that gave the Jews total religious freedom and judicial autonomy. *(To see how government laws are upheld in the realm of theft, see Section A, Law 5: "Stealing.")*

Yet those taxes clearly supported Babylonia's army for its self-preservation, as well as a police force that could preserve civil order according to the code of civil law upheld by its government. This fits in with another teaching of the Sages: *one should pray for the well-being of the ruling kingdom; for were it not for the fear of it, people would eat one another alive! (Mishnah, tractate Avoth 3:2)* They clearly recognized the legitimate roles governments play in enabling society to function.

It is therefore understood that non-Jews have the right to maintain a standing army for their self-preservation, to enact and enforce the basic civil laws that enable society to function — all in the context of enforcing the Seven Laws. *What is utterly forbidden, however, is capital punishment outside the context of the Seven Laws (which constitutes murder).* For example, for action forbidden by government legislation to be considered the capital crime of theft, *it must conform to the basic definition from the Torah – that personal property was physically taken from or withheld from its rightful owner.* Otherwise, although it may be penal in one's local system of civil law, it is not transgression of the Noahide Law.

Other forbidden abuses of power are unfair imprisonment, which constitutes the stealing of a human being (kidnap), and *any tax that would constitute thievery of the public.*

One must not confuse government with the commandment of establishing courts of justice. The seventh law restricts a court to punishing for violation of the Seven Laws only, and the means by which testimony is given, evidence established, conviction made, and penalty given out. This is a commandment which must be fulfilled everywhere. In the absence of any court, justice can even be administered by a single capable individual. *A government, on the contrary, is established voluntarily, based on the needs of a people within their domains.* So long as they are loyal to the Seven Laws, they are free to appoint their leadership by whatever

The Seven Noahide Commandments

means they see fit, and to enact any *civil* laws they believe will ensure their survival and prosperity. Moreover, these laws have the sanction of the Torah, so long as they do not contradict the Seven Laws.

h. The right to offer Temple sacrifices.

When the Holy Temple stands, any non-Jew – even an idolater – may give an `olah offering (a whole-burnt offering) to be offered on the altar. So long as the animal is found to be kosher, it will be offered by the kohen-priests. This can be a cow, sheep, goat, or pigeon. *(Ibid., Laws of Sacrificial Procedures 3:1)*

5. Regarding *Geruth Toshav* And Noahide Oaths:

Once the Jubilee year is restored, Noahides will be eligible to become *gere toshav* (resident aliens) by taking an oath before a panel of three Jews known for their dedication to ritual purity. Note that this does not merely entail taking an oath before three rabbis.

Moreover, until the status of *geruth toshav* is restored, no oath or verbal affirmation of one's loyalty to the Noahide Laws before Jews of any rank serves any *halakhic* (legal) purpose. Notwithstanding the rabbinical opinion that such an oath is what can enable a Noahide to have merit for keeping the Noahide laws; *Mishneh Torah* does not recognize any such prerequisite to the attaining the Heavenly reward that is promised all righteous human beings. *(Laws of Kings & Wars 8:14[11])* The Noahide who has made such an oath or statement — even before prominent rabbis — is no more a Noahide than one who has not.

* * * However, such a non-halakhic oath or statement made voluntarily can serves a positive, practical purpose so long as the Noahide understands its non-halakhic nature. It makes one clearly distinct from idolaters in the eyes of others. Moreover, it is a powerful social statement that encourages proper Noahide observance, and it is a sanctification of HaShem's Name.

Sadly, there are Noahides who, without mentioning names, relate to an oath before rabbis, an oath by a Torah scroll, or circumcision as the only means by which a non-Jew can achieve eternal life (the Life of the World to Come), or earn eternal reward for Torah observance. Although they have been misled to such ideas by Torah scholars, we understand that such Noahides and their teachers are not only placing artificial and non-existing limits on HaShem's compassion for righteous non-Jews, but those Noahides are thereby transgressing the rabbinical Noahide prohibition of adding religious customs and obligations which they deem to have the status of law. * * *

C
Cases of Exemption from the Noahide Laws and Punishment

1. Minors, the Insane and the Deaf

Minors include boys who have neither reached the age of 13 years and one day, nor show the physical sign of puberty *(8)*. For girls, a minor has neither reached 12 years and one day old, nor shows the physical sign of puberty. *Minors, the clinically insane, and the deaf-mute* (who can neither hear nor speak) *cannot be put to death for transgressing the Noahide Laws;* they are not held responsible for upholding the Commandments. *(Laws of Kings & Wars 10:3[2] cf. Book of Judges, Laws of Rebels 7:8[5])*

2. Cases of Coercion

For example, as explained above *(Section A, NoahideLaw #7)*, a non-Jew who violated the Noahide Laws under coercion is completely exempt from punishment. An example of this is rape: a Noahidess is not put to death if she were raped by anyone — Jew or non-Jew — *HaShem* forbid. A non-Jew is under no obligation to sanctify the Name of Heaven, which includes giving up one's life rather than transgressing *HaShem*'s Law. Even if he committed idolatry under threat of his life, he is exempt.

However, as stated above, ignorance of the law is not an acceptable excuse, and does not exempt a transgressor from punishment. Neither, does the threat of a lesser penalty or danger constitute coercion that would make one exempt.

3. In a Case of Doubt

Unlike Jews in regards to Torah Law (not rabbinical), Noahides have no obligation to be strict in a case of doubt. For example, if a non-Jew has reason to believe that the meat before him was *not* removed from a living animal (that ceased convulsing after death), he may eat it, even if considerable doubt still exists. *(Laws of Kings & Wars 10:1)*

What is considered "considerable doubt"? For example, according to my understanding, if it can be safely assumed that the majority of meat sold in a particular market place *is* kosher for Noahides; even if nearly 50% of the meat is suspected to be meat removed from a living animal, this is still not grounds for prohibiting meat of unknown origin from the market place.

* * * *We are not relating here to what may be ideal, only describing the letter of the law. Torah law for Israelites is much stricter in regards to meat with doubtful kosher status.* * * *

4. In Case of Unintentional Transgression

As mentioned above, if a non-Jew transgressed a Noahide commandment accidentally, he is exempt. This includes situations such as lying with another man's wife whom he believed to be unmarried, or lying with a Jewess whom he believed to be non-Jewish. In both cases, he is exempt. However, he cannot claim ignorance of the law. If he was aware of her status, but claimed he didn't know the law, he is still fully liable — just as one may not murder and claim he did not know murder was forbidden. *(Ibid. 2:1-2[1])*

5. Conversion to Judaism

Any non-Jew who transgressed any of the Seven Commandments but later converts to Judaism is exempted of his crimes. However, if he murdered an Israelite or committed adultery with a daughter of Israel (whether married or engaged), he is still held liable. For committing adultery with a betrothed woman, he is put to death by strangulation; if her marriage was already complete, he is liable to the same death penalty as if he had committed adultery with a non-Jewess: beheading by the sword. *(Laws of Kings & Wars 10:6[4])*

Although conversion exempts a Noahide of his past crimes, there is no turning back in the eyes of the Jewish court. Even if he wants to return to his status as a Noahide or resident alien (a Noahide permitted to live in Israel at the time when the Jubilee year is in force), any crimes he committed as a Jew are judged according to the Torah — not the Seven Noahide Commandments. *(Ibid. 10:4-5[3])*

The exceptions to this are non-Jewish children who were converted as minors — before the age of 13 for boys, before the age of 12 for girls. Before they reach those milestones that mark their coming of age *(8)*, they may rescind their conversion and return to their previous status as a Noahide or as a resident alien in Israel. However, after reaching those marks of adulthood; should they make the choice to continue to live as Jews, they too are not permitted to rescind thereafter – they are treated as full-fledged Israelites from that time forward. *(Ibid.)*

NOTES

(1) Passage below quoted from Faur, Jose (Bar Ilan University). *A Crisis of Categories: Kabbalah and Rise of Apostasy in Spain*, as printed in Lazar, Moshe & Haliczer, Stephen. *The Jews of Spain and the Expulsion of 1492*. Published by Labyrinthos, 1997: Lancaster, California. pp.41-53. Posted online at The José Faur

> A more devastating effect was accepting plurality as valid Jewish monotheism. It was further strengthened by those who maintained that the ten " mystical spheres" *(sefirot)* represent the very essence of God. Many had adopted the doctrine of R. Menahem Recanati (late thirteenth century-early fourteenth century), that prayers ought to be directed to a specific *sefira,* rather than to God Himself. Spanish mystics went into great intellectual contortions to explain how belief that the essence of God is made up of ten *sefirot* does not contradict Jewish monotheism.'**
>
> Referring to the doctrine of the ten *sefirot* expounded by R. Solomon ibn Adret, the famous mystic R. Abraham **Ablu'afya (1240-after 1291), remarked:**[147]
>
>> Accordingly, let me inform you that the masters of mysticism [and] the *sefirot* thought to profess the unity of God, and escape the doctrine of trinitarianism, and [in fact] they made him ten In the same fashion that the gentiles say "He is three and the three are one," some masters of mysticism say that the divinity is ten *sefirot* and the ten are one.
>
> It is clearly, therefore, the argument that "(Whereas) the Christians believe in the Trinity, the mystics believe in the Tentary (= ten *sefirot*)."[148]

Tora Studies Center, *www.josefaurstudies.org*

(2) This opinion is summarized in the following webpages: biblebelievers.org.au/moongod.htm; biblebelievers.org.au/islam.htm; posted to an idolatrous web source, the property of Yeshua Communications Network. Copyright 1997-8, All Rights Reserved. *www.yeshua.co.uk*.

(3) Flavius, Josephus, *The Wars of the Jews* (Translated by William Whiston), Hendrickson Publishers, Inc., Peabody Mass. 1987. 926 pp. *(Ch. 9:4, 380-381.)*

Truth to tell, this was taken from Josephus' propaganda speech to the Jews to lay down their weapons before the Romans, which contains a number of crude distortions. Nevertheless, *this description of Abraham at the head of a great army agrees with Oral tradition not only regarding the military might of Abraham, but his descendants — contrary to what is commonly taught.* Josephus slyly manipulates the story, painting Abraham as a pacifist — as if Abraham would have never resorted to a military solution if *HaShem* would not intervene with a miracle.

(4) See Rashi on *Genesis 32:9*. According to his commentary on 33:2, Jacob was prepared to take on Esau and his forces single-handedly if need be.

(5) Lehrman, Nathaniel S., M.D., *Homosexuality: Some Neglected Considerations* Originally published in: Journal of American Physicians and Surgeons Volume 10, Number 3 Fall 2005. Found online at: *www.jpands.org/vol10no3/lehrman.pdf*

(6) The website of *Jews Offering New Alternatives to Homosexuality*, found at: *www.jonahweb.org*

(7) Feuer, Rabbi Avrohom Chaim, *A Letter for the Ages (Iggeres HaRamban),* Mesorah Publications ltd., Brooklyn, NY 1996. 122 pp. *(See pages 37-38, the section entitled "Bittersweet Gifts.")*

(8) Besides arriving at the ages of 13 for boys and 12 for girls; the physical *halakhic* sign of the onset of adulthood for both boys and girls, for both Jews and non-Jews (according to their respective laws), is the sprouting of two pubic hairs. *(Book of Judges, Laws of Rebels 7:8[5])*

Guide for the Noahide

PART III

BEYOND THE LETTER OF THE LAW: THE COMMON DECENCY THAT *HASHEM* DESIRES OF NON-JEWS

Core universal values that, while not legal conditions
of the Noahide Covenant, are what
can allow humanity to reach its potential

הִשְׁתַּחֲווּ לַיהוָה בְּהַדְרַת קֹדֶשׁ,
חִילוּ מִפָּנָיו כָּל הָאָרֶץ.

(תהילים צו,ט)

Prostrate yourselves before YHWH*
in the splendor of holiness,
tremble before Him all the earth.

Psalms 96,9

* Not to be pronounced. This is read as the holy Name *'Adhonoy'* or the non-sacred term *HaShem,* which means literally "The Name."

Introduction To Part III

As we wrote in the introductory section, the Seven Noahide Laws are a beginning — the foundation — not an end. They are the minimal content by which a non-Jew — who observes them because *HaShem* commanded them through Moses at Sinai – earns the eternal life of the soul. They also define what is penal in a court of law and what is not, in order to avoid punishment by man. For example, in the freedom of thought afforded by the Noahide Laws, there is no outright, penal obligation (in this World) to believe there is a God. Therefore, while an atheist forfeits his portion in the World to Come; if he wishes to live a quiet life among Noahides — so long as he does not curse *HaShem* or commit idolatry — he could be an upstanding citizen, in principle. However, without a widespread belief and fear of *HaShem*, the Noahide system would quickly fall apart.

Another example: Technically speaking, a Noahide who lies left and right and shows only disdain for his parents cannot be prosecuted. However, how could a Noahide community survive as such from one generation to the next, if children are not taught to honor their parents? And without a strong value of honesty, how could there be unity or bonds of trust between individuals that make the society strong? *Clearly, human society cannot thrive without other key values.*

Ideally, all the values and character traits championed by the Torah are beneficial and important to mankind as a whole. However, there are some values that the Torah plainly shows to relate directly to Noahides, because they are lessons taken from the life examples of Noahides. In this section I will list these key values and explain their universal applicability.

Note that although they were already obligated to more than Seven Laws — particularly the commandment of circumcision *(Laws of Kings & Wars 9:3)* — the term "Noahide" applies equally to the progenitors of the Jewish people before the Giving the Torah at Sinai, as it does to righteous non-Israelites of the Bible (such as Jethro, Moses' father-in-law); all were obligated to the Noahide covenant. Even the antediluvians who lived before *HaShem*'s covenant with Noah were judged according to nearly the same system — the primordial Noahide Torah code of the Six Laws given to Adam. This only lacked the prohibition of consuming flesh taken from a living animal. *(Ibid 9:2[1])*

Fear of *Hashem*, Hearkening to the Prophet Who Speaks in His Name

Although there is no express commandment, it is clear that non-Jews are expected to fear *HaShem*. In the commandment to Israel to wipe out the memory of Amalek from under Heaven, *(Deut. 25:17-19)* the Torah recounts how they attacked the Israelites in the desert, noting *'and they didn't fear HaShem.'*

This entails awe for, and hearkening to the true prophet who speaks in His Name. For example, in Genesis 20:7, the pharaoh is commanded by *HaShem* to let Abraham's wife go *"for he is a prophet."* Although the pharaoh was being reprimanded by Heaven for his near-transgression of *adultery*, the Torah makes special emphasis on the fact that *Abraham is a prophet.*

We also learn this lesson from the long episode of Moshe's encounter with the wicked pharaoh of the Exodus. While the pharaoh was truly being dealt a drawn out Divine punishment for breaching the Noahide Laws of *murder* and *idolatry*; in the immediate context, the pharaoh's actions were being measured according to *whether or not he would hearken to the word of a true prophet of HaShem.*

It should be obvious that the city of Nineveh would not have been saved from *HaShem*'s wrath had they not hearkened to Jonah, the prophet who spoke in His Name.

Practically speaking, how can a society commit to the Noahide Covenant without fear and awe of the Lawgiver? For the individual, how can a person understand the dynamics of his world and his own place in it without awareness of the Creator, and the sheer fear and awe that evokes? Because of this it is written, "the beginning of wisdom is the fear of HaShem..." *(Psalms 111:10)*

Seeking Torah Guidance Of The Wise

The Torah teaches that during the travail that Rebecca underwent as her unborn twins struggled with one another from within her womb, she inquired of *HaShem*. According to Oral tradition, she visited the sages Shem and Ever *(Rashi on verse 25:22)*, who prophetically (in the Name of *HaShem*) told her about the two nations that were about to emerge: Israel and Edom *(Genesis 25:22-23)*. In fact, not only did Israel's progenitors (who were Noahides at the time) inquire of Shem and Ever in times of distress; we have a tradition that Abraham and Jacob actually studied under them in their early years. *(Sefer haYashar, parashoth Lekh Lekha and Toledoth)*

Although there is no Sanhedrin in our times, and the Seven Laws could theoretically be learned straight from *Mishneh Torah*; practically speaking, *how can Noahides know they have understood the law and its proper application without the counsel of properly trained Torah scholars?* At the same time, however, not all ordained rabbis are equipped to answer Torah questions in the field of the Noahide Laws. As much as Noahides must become fluent enough in the Law to fulfill it accurately, they should also establish a relationship with properly trained scholars who can remove their doubts and help settle their differences of opinion. However, as the practice of the Noahide Laws becomes more widespread, with more and larger communities being established, this will become more difficult.

Ultimately only the restoration of a true Sanhedrin will suffice to bring full clarity and unity on the difficult issues that will arise, as the world returns to the system of judgment that HaShem created for it. As quoted in the Introduction, the prophet Isaiah *(Isaiah 2:2-4)* presents a clear vision of this very phenomenon which will be commonplace in Messianic times:

> And it shall come to pass in the end of days, that the mountain of *HaShem*'s house will be established as the top of the mountains, and will be exalted above the hills; and all nations will stream to it. And many peoples will go and say: 'Come and let us go up to the mountain of *HaShem*, to the house of the God of Jacob; and He will teach us of His ways, and we will walk in His paths.' *For out of Zion shall go forth the Law, and the word of HaShem from Jerusalem.*

As explained previously, *HaShem*'s teachings going forth from "*HaShem*'s house" refers specifically to the holy judgment of the Sanhedrin, the "Pillar of Teaching" (*Mishneh Torah, Laws of Rebels ch.1*), when they will sit in the Chamber of Hewn Stone in the Temple. Their selfless work of righteous judgment will maintain a world at peace with its Creator and hence with itself, as it is written:

> And they shall beat their swords into plowshares, and their spears into pruninghooks; nation shall not lift up sword against nation, neither shall they learn war any more. *(Isaiah 2:4)*

Noahides —for their own benefit as much as the benefit of Jews— should act as a galvanizing force promoting the establishment of a true Sanhedrin according to *halakhah (codified practical law)*. To date, despite rumors and misinformation, no attempt to do so has succeeded in the last 1500 years.

Teaching One's Children

HaShem originally promised Abram (as Abraham was called before *HaShem* changed his name —*Genesis 17:5*) that the land in which he dwelled would be given *to him personally* as well as to his descendants, as it is written, "*to you* and to your seed after you forever." *(Gen. 13:14-17)* Although his progeny would be numerous as the dust of the earth, Abram was to inherit it in person, in his own lifetime. *HaShem* never makes empty promises. He brought about a large regional war from which Abram emerged as the sole conqueror, and rightful master of the land. Yet, in the aftermath of the war, Abram refused to supplant the wicked rulers of the land, to assume the mantle of leadership as "prophet-king" of the region. Instead, he left them alive to continue their abominable reigns of terror. Although he missed his chance to inherit the Land personally in his lifetime, *HaShem* comforted him, saying "Do not fear... your reward is very great" *(15:1)*, and renewed their Covenant. In this new covenant, Abram himself is not mentioned. Rather, he is told, "*...to your seed I have given this Land.*" (1)

It is then that Abram was given a terrifying vision of the future. Now, his progeny would be destined to sojourn and be tortured in a foreign land (the future slavery in Egypt). The very opening words in the Torah's account of this "Covenant Between the Pieces" *(15:1)* is "And it was after these things...", which always teaches that what is about to be taught is a direct result of what came just beforehand... In other words, this new future was the result —measure for measure— of what he had just failed to do. *Rather than taking possession of his own Land that HaShem had given him (by executing justice against the perversely wicked kings of the land — namely Sodom and Gomorrah), he continued to live like a stranger in his own land.*"

How did Abram merit *HaShem*'s great, unwavering love that survived this painful human blunder? In the Torah, *HaShem*

Himself tells us the reason for His great love of the God-fearing warlord:

> For I have loved him, to the end that he may command his children and his household after him, that they may keep the way of *HaShem*, to do righteousness and justice; to the end that *HaShem* may bring upon Abraham *[this is after God changed his name]* that which He hath spoken of him. *(Genesis 18:19)*

HaShem does not merely see where we are at a given time. He sees the future — what we are building, and where we are headed. Although Abraham *(again – after his name change)* had failed to establish *HaShem*'s kingship in the holy land in his own lifetime; *HaShem* saw how he would train his future sons, which vindicated the prophet in the eyes of the Holy One, Blessed be He.

The same is true with Noahides today. The success of the Noahide movement will not be defined by how successful they are in spreading the Noahide laws in this generation, but rather by the quality of the seeds they plant for the long-term future.

One lesson behind the ages of special individuals recorded in Genesis is *how long the ancients were ready to wait to see the prophesied fruit of their labors.* Noah waited 120 years between his prophecy of the Flood and its fulfillment. Abram was willing to wait ten years between his prophecy that he would father a nation, and his decision to take Hagar as a wife — since Sarai was barren. Had he waited 25 years until birth of Isaac, he would have realized there was no need to pre-empt *HaShem*'s promise. During the sojourn in Egypt, a contingent of warriors of Ephraim was unwilling to wait for the prophesied redemption at the end of 400 years (from the birth of Isaac). They met a disastrous fate in their premature attempt to conquer the Land. *(I Chronicles 7:20-22 cf. Midrash*

Rabbah Shir haShirim 2:7) How different might Israel's history have been if those men had remained to train their children in the traditions of Israel's forebears, in preparation for the true redemption only 30 years later? (For a rebuttal against those who use this source [as it is taught in *Talmud tractate Kethuboth 111a]* against religious Zionism, see Appendix II.)

Just like the Noahides of the ancient past, today's Noahides must be patient and mature to plan for the long term. *That means build their lives and communities on the core value of educating children in the uncompromising love and service of HaShem according to pure, authentic Torah Law.* Only thus can they be assured of a solid, bright and blessed future – even if it means giving up on the dream of a huge swell in numbers in the short term.

Honoring Parents

From the entire life stories of the original Noahides – the actual sons of Noah — *HaShem* chose only one single incident from their entire lives to be eternally recorded in the Torah. It is the episode when their father Noah became drunk, and lay naked in his tent. Shem and Japheth not only honored their father by covering his nakedness, but they did so in a way that would preserve his dignity: they walked *backwards* with their father's wrap on their shoulders to cover him, so they would not see their father shamefully exposed. *(Gen. 9:18-27)*

It was a defining moment not only in their lives, but for humanity. *By their action, they merited Noah's prophetic blessings for all their generations.* From this sole incident from the lives of the progenitors of humanity, we come to understand three things: (1) why this family was so special that they alone were saved, (2) how greatly important honoring parents is to *HaShem*, even though it is not an actual Noahide law, how we all, as their descendants, have the ability to rise up to that moral level. (3)

Conversely, when we consider the actions of Ham and the curse to his progeny through Canaan, we see how severe a crime it is to shame our parents – even when we feel they are behaving shamefully.

Many people are confused by the Torah's description of Ham's mockery of his naked father on one hand, and the fact that it is specifically his son Canaan who was cursed. While the commentaries abound with different theories and traditions over what Canaan's role may have been in the incident, the most profound explanation I've heard requires nothing more than the words of the account in Genesis.

When Noah's uttered "Cursed be Canaan; a servant of servants shall he be unto his brethren", what he meant was:

> This is how you treat your father, a prophet of *HaShem* in whose merit all humanity –including you— was saved from extinction?! *[Gen. 6:8, 7:1]* Poor Canaan is cursed. With a father such as you and an example such as yours, how will *he* become?! He is cursed!

The Idolater Who Became the Benchmark of Honoring Parents

The Talmud *(tractate Qidushin 31a)* relates two accounts of a gentile (apparently an idolater) by the name of Dama ben Nethinah, who lived in Ashkelon during the Second Temple era. This gentile is held up by the sages as the ultimate example of honoring parents. The *Kohen Gadol* (High Priest) was badly in need of precious stones for the Ephod, one of the sacred garments of the High Priest. Knowing that Dama owned the very stones that were required, the Jewish Sages made their way to Ashkelon to purchase them from him, offering him 600,000 dinar (800,000 according to another opinion). But no matter how much they offered, the gentile firmly refused: *His father was sleeping, and the key to the chest of gems lay under his father's pillow and he would not disturb him for any sum of money.* The following year, HaShem blessed Dama with the ultimate treasure: a red heifer was born in his herd. When the sages came to him, he told them modestly,

> I know about you [Jews] that I could ask you for all the money in the world and you would give it, but I only ask for the amount of money that I lost for [my] father's honor. *(Qidushin 31a)*

From this story we learn how *HaShem* rewards even a non-Jew for honoring his parents, even though non-Jews are not expressly commanded regarding the honor of parents.

The Price Jacob Paid For Deceiving His Father

Contrast this with how the patriarch Jacob suffered time and again in his life for deceiving his old, blind father Isaac, *even though he did so to honor his mother's request.*

At the beginning of Genesis 27, the family seemed to be at the brink of imminent disaster. The blind father had just invited his godless son Esau to prepare to receive the patriarchal blessing, which would normally have made him the inheritor of the land and master to his brothers. Only at the urging of his mother Rebecca did Jacob begrudgingly agree to deceive his father, in order to avoid this potential catastrophe. However, *despite* his noble intentions, *despite* the fact that Noahides are neither obligated by law to honor their parents, nor prohibited from lying (especially in such a desperate situation), and *despite* that fact that Esau had formally and legally sold his birthright (along with the patriarchal blessing that accompanied it), *HaShem still repaid Jacob measure for measure for what he did to his father, throughout his life.* Time and again throughout the rest of his life, we see him deceived and shocked in just the same way he deceived and shocked his father.

For example, after seven years of hard labor under the most difficult conditions, Laban deceives him, replacing Rachel, his youngest daughter whom Jacob loved, with Leah, his eldest daughter. By the time Jacob realizes he has been deceived, it is too late — the marriage has already been consummated. And what are Laban's words to Jacob? "And Laban said: 'It is not so done in our place, to give the younger before the firstborn.'" *We see that just as Jacob, the younger sibling, had deceived his blind father by pretending to be the eldest, whom his father loved; so too was he deceived while he was blind (in the darkness of night) with the eldest daughter, instead of the younger sibling whom he loved.*

Years later, Jacob has a favorite son of his own — Joseph. After Joseph's brothers kidnap him and sell him into slavery, they return home to deceive their father —just as Jacob had deceived Isaac — telling him that Joseph had been devoured by a wild animal. In the original deception, Jacob had disguised himself as Esau in *clothing of goat skin (27:16)*, as the Torah writes, "And he [Isaac] did not *discern him [wa-lo 'hikiro']* because his hands were hairy, like his brother Esau's hands; so he blessed him." *(27:23)* Note the same wording when Jacob's sons present him with *Joseph's coat dipped in goat blood:* "and they sent the coat of many colors, and they brought it to their father; and said: 'This have we found. *Discern* now *('haker' na)* whether it is your son's coat or not.'" *(37:32)*

It was a message to Jacob, and it remains a lesson to all humanity, for all time: First, that the ends do not always justify the means; second, that slighting the honor of a virtuous parent is not something *HaShem* takes lightly. This should be something that does not require a formal law to understand. Fittingly, when a non-Jew converts to Torah

Judaism, he then becomes obligated by law to honor his idolatrous parents.

Respect For Women And Modesty

Beth Avraham, the house of Abraham, was a flowering Noahide community of "souls they had made in Haran" *(Genesis 12:5)* — people he had converted away from idolatry to the true faith. Surely among these many families of servants and students of the prophet-warlord, there must have been young girls for Isaac to marry. Yet incomprehensibly, Abraham had his eyes set on the family he had left behind in *Aram Naharayim*, who remained idolaters. If Laban's behavior is indicative of their values, they would be no strangers to lying, cheating and theft. *What was there in Aram that convinced Abraham that the root of his dynasty could only be found there?* In the Torah, which is usually sparse on detail, this story is described in vivid detail for a reason. In perspective of all the stories of Laban, from Abraham's time to Jacob, it becomes clear that the house of Bethuel was a home in which women were not only cared for and protected, *but where they were also respected as intelligent human beings.*

Despite the riches that would be theirs from such a contract, the family is not hasty in permitting Rebecca to become betrothed to Isaac. Rather, they do a rare thing for those days — they ask the girl's opinion:

> And her brother and her mother said: 'Let the girl reside with us for a year or ten months; after that she may go.' And he said to them: 'Do not delay me, seeing that *HaShem* has made my mission succeed; send me off so I may go to my master.' And they said: *'We will call the girl and ask her opinion.' (24:55-57)*

Here we see that Rebecca's intelligence was respected; she was not being treated as a mere object to be married off. Their parting blessing to her also carries the message of their high regard and hopes for her:

> And they blessed Rebecca, and said to her: 'Our sister, may you be the mother of thousands of ten thousands, and *may your offspring possess the gate of their enemies.*' *(24:60)*

This pattern continues to hold true even later in the story of Rachel and Leah. This puts the stormy relationship between Laban and Jacob in an interesting, new light. Pushing Leah into marriage with Jacob might well have been Laban's way of saving her from the fate of marrying the wild and godless Esau. When Laban pursues and overtakes Jacob in his flight homeward, consider the opening words of Laban's scourging attack, and then his final parting message to Jacob:

> And Laban said to Jacob: 'What have you done, that you deceived me, and *carried away my daughters as though captives of the sword?* Why did you flee secretly... and didn't leave me to kiss my sons and my daughters.... *(31:26-28)*

> *[Promise] that you will not ill-treat my daughters, and that you will not take wives beside my daughters,* no man being with us; see — God is witness between me and you.' *(31:50)*

Blind to his own selfishness and unfairness, Laban sees in Jacob's action his worst nightmare — that his daughters be carried off as captives of war. He is deeply emotional about losing them. Yet, despite his character flaws, *I believe that his zealous caring for them is the very quality that made his home the root of the nascent Hebrew nation.*

In order to appreciate how rare that must have been in those times, consider how latent and widespread child abuse is today, even in a world infused with basic, watered-down Torah principles through the religions it spawned. (A teaching of RaMBaM regarding the temporary role that Christianity and Islam have played in *HaShem*'s world can be found in *Laws of Kings & Wars 11:11*.) Considering the dreadful state of affairs in our times when there are prohibiting laws, one can only imagine how rampant child abuse of every kind must have been in *those* times — especially the abuse of girls. To this day, there are traditional societies in which girls are viewed chiefly as objects of family wealth to be married off for a good bride price.

Attitudes such as these do not end with the perpetrators; they are passed on to the victims. Modern statistics show that children who were abused themselves are far more likely to abuse their own offspring. Perhaps that is the reason Abraham couldn't entrust his beloved son to a girl from the families he had converted to the Torah of Noah and Shem. In a world where life for most women was, in the words of Thomas Hobbes, "poor, nasty, brutish and short", the house of Bethuel would have been a special exception.

In a world culture in open revolt against traditional values, this message couldn't be more critical for our own homes in these times.

Modesty: For the Sake of a Woman's Dignity, Her Family, and the Noahide Laws

Among the most tragic victims of the crooked values of world culture, are women — and along with them the family. Women are objectified in a most sinister way. Through media and liberal arts education, *they are fooled into thinking that by exposing more of their body, they become empowered and dignified.*

The Torah teaches that when Rebecca saw Isaac for the first time, she did not move to expose more of herself; on the contrary — *to appear more dignified, she covered herself with a veil. (Genesis 24:65)* This is part of the Torah principle of "all the honor of the daughter of the king is on the inside." *(Psalms 45:14,* as discussed in *Book of Women, Laws of Marriage 13:14)* In fact, in all the accounts about royal dress through the ages that I have read or heard of, royalty are always more covered up than the lay public.

One striking exception is the account of Ahasuerus, King of Persia, from the book of Esther. Wanting to show off his wife's beauty, the Persian king ordered that his wife Vashti appear nude before his dinner party, wearing nothing but her royal crown. *(Book of Esther 1:11, cf. Talmud, tractate Meghillah 12b)* According to the mentality of today's "liberated woman", what had the queen to lose? She was the most powerful woman in the kingdom, in her husband's home, protected by the royal guard — *of what was there to be afraid?* Her external beauty must have been exquisite for the king to make such a request — *of what was there to be ashamed?* Surely, many lower-ranking women with the attitude of "if you've got it, show it", would have loved to take her place.

However, it appears that Vashti did not share the cheap mentality of the low class. Born into royalty — the granddaughter of Nebuchadnezzar — she may have well understood that immodesty is humiliating. Perhaps it was out of an inability to bear such humiliation that she refused. According to Talmud *(Ibid.),* she had personally done this same thing to Jewish women under her charge: in order to shame them, she had ordered them to work on the Sabbath day stark naked. *Vashti's refusal was tantamount to suicide.* When she refused to accept the "regal honor" to do as she had commanded her Jewish servant girls, she was promptly deposed, and — according to Rashi's commentary on the above Talmudic source— put to death.

Regardless of what a woman is aware of, what she may imagine to herself about how others see her, or her cultural expectations of how men *should* behave; human nature will never change. In truth, decent, God-fearing men who are modest themselves will rise above their animal natures and see her for the person she is. But most men — including otherwise good, well intending fellows — will fall short, reacting according to what their senses pick up. *The level of a woman's modesty in the way she dresses, moves and speaks, sends a powerful message to the men around her as to how they should relate to her:*

- according to her blinding, physical female charm, or according to the human being she is inside...
- as a single, available woman, or as a committed wife and mother...
- as a woman who chooses to play naïve about men's nature, or as one who is caring enough not to place a 'stumbling block before the blind'...

That being said, I will not go as far as to suggest that Noahide woman should feel compelled to cover their hair, or that there should be separate seating between men and women at Noahide gatherings. To our understanding, *outside the specific mandates of the Torah for Jews; what is considered modest is relative according to one's culture.* What is considered dignified and modest in California is not what would be considered dignified and modest in Kuwait. We understand that was left open without legislation — neither by *HaShem* nor by the rabbis — can be just as significant as what was explicitly commanded. To add to the law is no better than detracting from it. *(Deut. 13:1)*

The principle of modesty for *both women and men* — according to the norms of the society in which one lives — is a must for any healthy Noahide society that hopes to guard itself against the rampant infringement of the laws of forbidden sexual intercourse, and preserve the institution of the family.

Marriage & Family Versus A 'Planet Of The Apes'

To Live As A Complete Human Being

The Talmud states:

> A man who does not have a wife lives without joy, without blessing, and without goodness. In the West they said, "Without Torah and without moral protection." Rabba ben Ulla said: "And without peace." *(tractate Yevamoth 62b)*

They were simply expanding on the simplest, most profound statement by *HaShem* Himself: *"It is not good for man to be alone; I will make for him a helper equivalent to him." (2:18)*

Consider the very first verse relating to man's creation, Genesis 1:27, a friend related to me the following profound observation on the verse:

> And God created the human in His own likeness, in the likeness of God He created him; male and female He created them. (2)

A human as a whole concept is defined as both male and female. An unmarried man is therefore, in a sense, only "half" a complete human being. This understanding is certain to upset many single people, but it is clear to anyone blessed with a life partner who is truly a "helper who is his equivalent." It is upsetting to them for the very reason the well-known Jewish American talk-show host Dennis Prager noted in his audio tape commentary to Genesis. (3) *The Torah does not teach that man felt lonely.* It is reasonable to assume that, among the animals, Adam was oblivious to the fact he was, on a deep existential level, alone. On the contrary, single men — more often than not — do not feel lacking. Free to roam, they do not comprehend what they are missing out on. Prager then cites a statistic that over 80% of the violent crime in the world is perpetrated by single men... *It is in His perfect Wisdom who understands that it is not good for man to be alone.*

Western 'Culture of the Apes' Versus Universal Traditional Wisdom

I add: *If it is not good for man to be alone, it is especially not good for him to be alone in his youth.* Despite the claims of social scientists and high school 'state requirements' teachers; young couples (Noahides as much as Jews) must be given the opportunity, should they so choose, to marry in their early teens. While it is easier for those in a segregated, parochial school system; for the vast majority of the young generation, the natural and societal pressures are too strong to resist. At just the age when they hardly bear the thought of squelching their God-given drive — their need to have intimate relations — until they are 18 years old, they are taught the ways of contraception as part of their school curriculum. As part of this secular Western education, they are taught — with the help of the media — that we are nothing more than "thinking apes"; an equation that carries clear sexual ramifications. (4) Fittingly, they learn to live like bonobo chimpanzees — treating intimacy like profane, regular social interaction. (5) If the teens are from a traditional culture, it becomes their form of rebellion, having secret relations like thieves in the night. Because of this cruel choice forced upon adolescents, an untold number of inner-city children are born into broken homes. *Thus, a new, lost generation is growing up without parental role models. Without the know-how to one day build solid marriages themselves, they are left with little choice but to pass on their ape-culture to their own young.* This is also one of the major factors promoting abortion — which for Noahides, in the majority of cases, is plainly murder.

In short, while the human evolution dogma, in which the world's youth are indoctrinated, teaches that man rose from the apes, it seems to be having the opposite effect. From post-modern generation to generation, it is bringing man down to the morality of the apes.

Until the invasion of Western culture relatively recently in history, every traditional culture recognized a basic Torah principle: *the right of young people to live together as man and wife from the onset of puberty, while still under the protection of their parents' roof.* The sooner the non-Jewish world embraces this natural, age-old solution; the sooner abortion rates will fall, teenage delinquency will fall, and young women will be seen less and less by men merely as opportunities for illicit sexual relations.

the War On the Multi-Generational Family

What do the world's political and business elite stand to gain from what translates to a war on the institution of family? That is simple. The family has always been, from time immemorial, the basic institution for passing on cultural knowledge and tradition. In order for the modern state and its values to replace the ancient traditions of the families of the earth, the institution of the multi-generational family must gradually be done away with. *World pop culture is accomplishing just this task.*

To preserve the sacred institution by which Torah values are passed on to future generations, *Noahides should make every effort to prepare their children to assume their role as responsible, dedicated parents and spouses at what is considered an early age in today's world.* That is by training them with the skills necessary to provide a modest living for themselves and by *limiting their exposure to popular culture — namely entertainment —* to whatever degree possible and practical.

Truthfulness And Repentance

Without citing examples, the "greatness" of the heroes of ancient non-Jewish myth, stems from their being of divine or noble birth. Since they are perfect from birth, they do not grow or change — and that is the very proof of the falsehood in those stories. *The greatness of Israel's forebears is how they rise from lowly birth (either as slaves or of ignoble ancestry) or from the errors of their youth, to strive for perfection.* Immortalized in the accounts of the Torah, their lives are models HaShem has given the world — both Jews and Noahides — to learn from.

Jacob was one Noahide who is related to in rabbinical literature as the very paragon of truth. Considering what we learned previously in *Honoring Parents*, how could this be? *How did it come to be?*

Jacob's Rise to Become the Paragon of Truth

With the maturity Jacob gained over the years while he was away from his family, he makes a clear break from his old self. At his initial act of reunion with his brother Esau, even before they embrace, he prostrates to him seven times (seven being a number symbolizing completion). Then, in the ensuing conversation, *he hints that he is giving Esau back the blessing* he obtained by ill-begotten means:

> *Please take my blessing ['birkhathi'] that was brought to you because God hath dealt graciously with me, and because I have everything.' And he urged him, and he took it. (Genesis 33:11)*

Clearly, Jacob is referring on a mundane level to his tribute to Esau — the physical gifts that he had sent ahead of him to appease his brother. However, nowhere in the Bible is a material gift or tribute from one person to another called *berakhah*, or "blessing." The word for tribute is *minhhah*. An excellent example of a similar gift of appeasement in the era of the patriarchs (by Jacob himself) is the special gift that Jacob sent back to Egypt with his sons to appease the prime minister, who unbeknownst to him was Joseph. As it is written *(43:11)*:

> And their father Israel said to them: 'If it be so now, do this: take of the choice fruits of the land in your vessels, and carry down the man a tribute *[minhhah]*, a little balsam, and a little honey, gum and resin, pistachio nuts and almonds.

The same language is used later in the chapter *(43:24-25)*:

> And the man brought the men into Joseph's house, and gave them water, and they washed their feet; and he gave feed to their donkeys. And they prepared the tribute *[minhhah]* until Joseph's arrival at noon; for they heard that they would eat bread there.

For other translations of *minhhah*: The Jerusalem Bible *(Koren 1992)* has it translated as "a present", and Aryeh Kaplan "a gift" *(The Living Torah,* Moznaim 1981) All connotations of gift-giving are covered. Clearly, Jacob's unique use of the word *birkhathi* to Esau — "take my blessing" refers to something else. In view of Jacob's seven prostrations and his firm insistence that Esau take the "blessing" (not a "tribute", "gift", or "present"), Jacob's intent becomes clear. He was symbolically returning what was his for the taking (*birkhathi* = "*my blessing*" — for Jacob had legally purchased the birthright and the patriarchal blessing that came with it), *because he had received their father's blessing through deceit.*

Esau treats it purely as a material gift and does not view or accept it as an actual return of the blessing. He returns to his new home in the land of Seir, leaving the coveted land to Jacob and his progeny. To my understanding, this event lies at the root of why Jacob is referred to, in rabbinical literature, as the paragon of truth.

There are two notable results of Jacob's action. The first is that now *HaShem* Himself crowns him with the patriarchal blessing, naming him the successor of Abraham and Isaac. *(35:11-12)* Perhaps this was to reward Jacob and reaffirm the blessing that Jacob was willing to return with no thought to his personal honor. Secondly, the very next section of the Torah opens with the birth of Esau's nation, Edom — his every son becoming a tribal chieftain, no less. Perhaps this was due to the influence of the blessing that Jacob so bravely returned to him.

How One Noahide's Truthfulness Became the Root of the Redemption of Mankind

In Genesis 38, we find an example of how *one Noahide's truthfulness — even at the price of self degradation — became the very foundation of the world's ultimate redemption.* That Noahide is Judah, son of Jacob.

When Judah inadvertently had relations with his own daughter-in-law (after her husband had died), causing her to conceive, it was a great personal embarrassment. Although such behavior is not forbidden to Noahides *(Book of Women, Laws of Marriage 1:4)*, such behavior was beneath the higher standard expected of the Hebrews, especially since Judah was expected to give Tamar to his son Shelah. Yet, rather than hide from his humiliation, Judah takes full responsibility: "And Judah identified them, and said: *'She is more righteous than I*; forasmuch as I gave her not to Shelah my son.' And he knew her again no more." *(38:26)*

Because of Judah's integrity, Tamar survived the ordeal, giving birth to twins: Peretz and Zerah. Peretz was the ancestor of King David, and the future Messiah-king. *(I Chronicles 2:4-15)*

It could be said that in the merit of his integrity, Judah merited a descendent that would become the symbol of honesty and repentance to the world — a mighty king who would immediately humble himself before *HaShem* and man, admitting guilt to a horrible crime... King David. The entire incident of Judah and Tamar foreshadows King David's liaison with Bathsheba. After the king is confronted by Nathan the prophet for his misdeed with her, King David — just like his righteous ancestor — takes full responsibility: "And David said to Nathan: 'I have sinned against *HaShem.*'" *(Samuel II, 12:13)*

The discerning Torah student can now perceive that Judah's integrity was the very seed of honesty and repentance that would be the hallmark of King David. What an example to today's political leaders. In a world in which mankind's arrogance and deceit seem to know no bounds, these values of honesty and repentance are the seeds of redemption.

Honesty And Respect In Marriage

Another Lesson From the Deception of Isaac

Honoring parents is not the only message in the story of the deception of Isaac. There is another key character in the story — Rebecca. The way the Torah relates to the deception of Isaac teaches us much about honesty and respect in marriage.

As explained above, Jacob only begrudgingly agreed to his mother's request, out of fear that he could be cursed, rather than blessed. Notably she does not reply that there would be no reason for a curse to come upon Jacob. Rather, she takes full personal responsibility for the curse to come: "And his mother said unto him: *'Upon me will be your curse, my son*; only hearken to my voice, and go fetch me them.'" *(27:13)* Notably, unlike all the other forefathers and foremothers of Israel, neither Rebecca's death nor her burial are given any mention in the Torah. To drive home the point, the passing of Rebecca's wet-nurse, Deborah, *is* mentioned: "And Deborah, Rebecca's nurse, died, and she was buried below Beth-el under the oak; and the name of it was called *Allon-bokhuth*." *(35:8) The clear lesson to be gained is that deception in marriage carries a heavy price.*

The Choice Between The Pit Of Depression And A Life Of Joy

The Cain Who Chose to Wallow In Depression and Faithlessness

What brought Cain, who brought one of the first offerings to *HaShem* in history, to spiral down to the point he would murder his only brother? This is not merely an academic question. In our times, *the malaise Cain suffered from has spread throughout the Western world like an epidemic — it's called DEPRESSION.* After his offering to HaShem was rejected in favor of Abel's offering, the Torah records:

> ...but to Cain and his offering *[HaShem]* paid no heed. *Cain was furious and depressed* [lit. "his face fell"]. *And HaShem said to Cain: 'Why are you furious? Why are you depressed? If you improve yourself, you can become great. But if you do not improve yourself, sin is crouching at the door and it lusts after you, but you can dominate it. And Cain spoke to Abel; and it came to pass when they were in the field Cain rose up against his brother and slew him.* (6) *(Genesis 4:5-8)*

Jealous and angry of his brother's favor in *HaShem*'s eyes, Cain allowed himself to sink into deep depression. Ignoring *HaShem*'s kind counsel to him, the world's first farmer murdered his brother, 'sowing the seeds' for the world's destruction — a world of violence that brought on the Flood. But even after his crime, neither Cain's fate nor the fate of the world was sealed. *HaShem* still gave Cain the opportunity to repent, commanding that he live the non-materialistic life of a nomad. *(4:12)*

HaShem knew that by giving up a life of permanent settlement (by which one is drawn to amass material possessions) Cain could guard himself and his descendants against jealousy and hate. At the root of his jealousy was a lack of trust in *HaShem*'s judgment. *Learning to trust and depend on HaShem for his sustenance, as a nomad does, he could finally achieve true happiness — which comes from knowing that all depends on HaShem, and ultimately all is for the best.*

Instead, Cain chooses to wallow in his misery, claiming "my sin is too great for me to bear." *(4:13)* Not trusting in the protection *HaShem* gave him, he fears for his life, and proceeds to do the *precise opposite* of what *HaShem* had commanded him: he settles down to build the world's first city. *(4:17) In the end, with the exception of Naamah* (Rashi on Gen. 4:22), *his progeny were wiped out all with the world of violence he helped create.*

For the Noahide as much as for the Jew, the ultimate root of depression is a lack of faith in *HaShem's* wisdom and judgment. It is the road to apostasy.

The 'Cain' Who Chose the Route of Joy and Faith

Contrast Cain with Jethro, the father of the Midianite clan called the *Qenim* (Kenites). *The prophet Bil`am actually calls them "Qayin" — the name of Cain himself (Numbers 24:22).* In what way could they be associated with Cain? They lived the simple, nomadic lifestyle that *HaShem* prescribed for Cain. Far into the future, the prophet Jeremiah is commanded by *HaShem* to invite a Kenite family, the Rechabites, to the Holy Temple, to serve them wine. Yet the Rechabite Kenites politely refuse:

> But they said: 'We will drink no wine; for Jonadab the son of Rechab our father commanded us, saying: You shall drink no wine, neither you, nor your sons, forever; *neither shall you build a house, nor sow seed, nor plant a vineyard, nor have any; rather, all your days you shall dwell in tents, so that you may live many days in the land in which you sojourn.* And we have hearkened to the voice of Jonadab the son of Rechab our father in all that he charged us... not to build houses for us to dwell in, neither to have a vineyard, or a field, or seed; but we have dwelt in tents, and have hearkened, and done

according to all that Jonadab our father commanded us.' *(Jeremiah 35:6-10)*

The Kenites are called after the name of Cain, for they undertook to fulfill *HaShem*'s mandate to Cain. In fact, *from the life of their ancestor Jethro, the entire Kenite mindset was one of choosing right in every place that Cain had chosen wrong:*

As we know, rather than rejoicing in his brother's favor before *HaShem*, rejoicing and trusting in *HaShem*'s judgment, Cain became angry, jealous and sad. When Jethro heard about the redemption of the Israelites from Egypt — particularly the splitting of the Red Sea — the Torah records, "*And Jethro rejoiced for all the goodness which HaShem had done to Israel*, in that He had delivered them out of the hand of the Egyptians." Lauding *HaShem*'s fairness in punishing the Egyptians measure for measure, Jethro – a non-Jew — blessed *HaShem*, recognized His Omnipotence, and then brought offerings to Him.

In the merit of this joyful recognition of *HaShem* and brotherly love to the Israelites, he and his progeny would become a part of Israel's eternity. *Jethro's progeny would remain as eternal as the Jewish People, with their own inheritance in the Land of Israel forever.* If the oral tradition of today's Druze is to be believed, we can perceive how *HaShem* has indeed remained faithful to this promise — for they would be the descendants of Kenites. To this day, this deeply monotheistic people remain residents of the land of Israel, and many have given their lives defending the Jewish people in the modern state of Israel.

For the Noahide as much as for the Jew, rejoicing with full faith in HaShem's judgment, and depending on Him alone for our sustenance, are the keys to true joy and eternal life.

Refraining From Cruel Anger

Anger is such an awful character trait, that the Sages likened one who becomes enraged to an idolater. *(Mishneh Torah, Laws of Character Traits 2:7[3])* Whoever loses his temper – unable to accept that on some level, whatever happens is part of *HaShem*'s Will — has in a sense, during those moments, denied *HaShem*'s rulership of the world. Furthermore, nothing will stop a person who acts out of rage. No matter what he may believe about himself at the time, he has to some degree — even if temporarily — thrown off the yoke of the Kingdom of Heaven.

Besides the story of Cain and Abel, there is another classical Torah example of cruel anger that resulted in the taking of human life — and it is one of the most poorly understood events in the Bible... It is the anger of Shimon and Levi in their conquest of Shechem. *The most common misunderstanding is that the patriarch Jacob was against a surprise attack on Shechem.* On the contrary, the conquest of the city by his sons Shimon and Levi became the textbook example of the execution of Noahide justice against a city or nation that refuses to bring criminals to justice. RaMBaM teaches as follows:

> This is why all the people of Shechem were liable for the death penalty: For behold, Shechem stole and they saw; they knew and they did not bring him to justice. And a Noahide can be executed with one witness and with one judge. *(Book of Judges, Laws of Kings & Wars 9:19)*

Not only did Israel's sages of blessed memory learn practical law from Shimon and Levi's vengeance against Shechem, but a close reading of the patriarch's blessings reveals that *it was their cruel anger that was cursed, not their deed:*

> Cursed be their <u>anger,</u> for it was fierce, and their <u>wrath</u>, for it was cruel; I will divide them in Jacob, and scatter them in Israel. *(Genesis 49:7)*

What was cursed was the hot rage of Shimon and Levi, which characterized the act as one of personal vengeance, rather than an act purely for HaShem's honor. Had they sat in judgment with their brothers and taken the counsel of their father, they could have devised a better-planned, better-coordinated attack, and taken steps to prevent reprisals by the surrounding Amorite kings. *(See the Aluf Abir's understanding below. Note: According to Oral tradition, with the exception of Joseph and Benjamin, who were still young, every son of Jacob was already a master warrior at the time [Sefer haYashar, parashath Wayishlahh]).*

In truth, the Patriarch was so proud of the conquest on Shechem, that on his death bed, when he bequeathed the city to his son Joseph, he spoke as if the city had been conquered by his own hand: *"Moreover I have given you one portion — Shechem — above what I have given your brothers, that which I took from the hand of the Amorite with my sword and with my bow."* (Genesis 48:22)

However, if the Hebrew word *hhamas*, which can be synonymous with "outrage", is better translated as "violence", *wouldn't Jacob be clearly understood to be condemning the violence?* (7) His rebuke opens thus: *"Shimon and Levi are brothers; their swords are <u>weapons of violence</u> ['hhamas']."* This is a classical example of how perilous Torah study in a foreign translation can be. Rather than using the noble Hebrew word for sword (*hherev*), Jacob "cursed" their swords using the Greek term for sword — '*mekher.*' *(Rashi on verse 49:5)*

To my understanding, the observation of the Aluf Abir Yehoshua Sofer-Ma`atuf Dohh, according to a tradition of the

Bani Abir clan of Habbani Jewry, is the key to the solution. He teaches:

> Yaaqov Avinu [Jacob our forefather] curses their sword using the Greek word *Mekher* to accentuate his perception of their action — *putting their faith in a sword like a Greek as opposed to exacting justice with Hebrew faith in all that is right and just.* They assumed the might in their hands in the form of their weapon would certainly be enough and this blinded them; bringing danger upon themselves and their brothers.
>
> The Habbani tradition is that although they angered their father by their reckless action, we fully feel for and embrace their warrior spirit and the nobility of their action and we praise them. *(from private correspondence)*

It was as if Jacob said thus: "Their swords, which they wielded out of impulsive anger like Greek-idolaters, became weapons of *violence* — instead of weapons of *justice.*"

Ultimately, out of the same impulsive anger — a trait befitting idolaters of the time — *they took similar vengeance on their own innocent brother Joseph.* Blinded by anger, they lost the ability to give the benefit of the doubt when it was required. They convinced themselves that their young, dreamy-eyed brother was a rising demagogue among them — the Ishmael or Esau of their generation. The key role that Shimon played in the sale of Joseph *(Sefer haYashar, parashath Wayyeshev)* becomes clear years later. When the brothers made their first trip to Egypt to buy grain, it was none other than Shimon that Joseph imprisons. It was so fitting that he should be one singled out, that the brothers realized that it must be a sign of Divine punishment for the sale and assumed death of Joseph. *(Genesis ch. 42)*

For Noahides as much as for Jews, careful and exacting performance of *HaShem's* commandments requires careful, deliberate and rational judgment; knowing as much when to wage war as when to apply mercy and give the benefit of the doubt. *Anger makes such judgment impossible.*

Kindness And Hospitality

Abraham's nephew Lot is a perfect example of the reward and Divine protection that comes from kindness and hospitality to others. As imperfect as he was (being ready to sacrifice his daughters to a mob of gang-rapists), he tried to provide safe haven for visitors at great risk to his own life. In this merit (as well as the merit of Abraham, of course), he alone was saved from the Divine punishment of Sodom and Gomorrah.

That this basic human kindness is expected of non-Jews is evident in the Torah Commandment to distance the Moabite and Ammonite from *ever* marrying into the Jewish People (after conversion). *(Deut. 23:4-5, cf. Book of Holiness, Laws of Forbidden Sexual Relations 12:14[18])* In that commandment, the Torah gives the reason: *"because they did not meet you with bread and water on the way, when you came forth out of Egypt..."*

In many ways, we live in a world that seems to be falling apart at the seams. This time, in which the numbers of new jobless and homeless families are soaring, can bring out the worst in people. In what is otherwise a book of core Torah principles based purely on Bible, *Mishneh Torah*, and a few sources from Talmud, I find nothing more fitting to illustrate the role of kindness in the world than one old Hassidic parable. *(Its purpose, of course, is not to attempt to accurately relate to us what the soul actually undergoes after death, but to teach a moral lesson.)*

Once, when a certain man passed away, his departed soul ascended for Judgment before the Heavenly scales. But after all his life deeds and sins were weighed before him, they were found to be perfectly even. He was therefore given a unique opportunity to see both *Gan 'Eden* (Heaven) and Gehinnom (Hell), that he might choose where he would prefer to be.

At first he was taken down to Gehinnom. He was amazed when he beheld the luxury in which the souls in Gehinnom lived — sitting around stately tables filled with finest, most exquisite, mouth-watering foods and drinks. Perhaps Gehinnom should be his choice, he thought. But he was shocked to see that the souls were starving. He could not understand how they could be starving amidst such a feast, until he noticed something odd: the souls had only stiff wooden forks and spoons for arms. Try as they may, they could not succeed by any means to bring the food to their mouths!

He asked to be shown *Gan 'Eden*. How surprised he was to see the same scene! Seated around stately tables, the souls of the righteous were sitting with only stiff wooden forks and spoons for arms. How was this any better than Gehinnom, he thought? Yet when he looked closer, he noticed that the souls looked well-fed and sated. Why? What was different? Then he noticed the reason: *the souls in Gan 'Eden were feeding each other.*

The difference between a world that is like hell and a world that is heavenly is not in the standard of living, or in the level of technology. *Rather, the principle difference is in how people choose to relate to one another.* As the world unifies more and more into a "New World Order"; Noahides, as much as Jews, have the opportunity to make it a world of *hhesed* — of loving-kindness — even if only for their own families and communities. A world of generosity, mutual respect, giving the benefit of the doubt, engendering unity, etc... If such a spirit is engendered, preserved and guarded properly, making it a light to the masses of humanity in this global village, how can authentic Noahide observance do anything but spread?

Blessing And Standing By The Jewish People And Recognizing Their Role In History

Another Great Lesson From Jethro

The classic positive Torah example of this value is Jethro. Although it can be demonstrated that he became reunited with Moshe, his son-in-law, only *after* the Giving the Law at Sinai, the account of their joyous reunion is recorded *immediately* following the account of the battle with Amalek *(Exodus 17:1-16)*. The Sages teach that this is to juxtapose Amalek's reaction to the Splitting of the Sea (to destroy the Israelites), with that of Jethro (to support and attach himself to them). Jethro's contributions to Israel are eternally enshrined in the Torah: his gift of a justice system *(Exodus 18:13-26)*, and his serving as their 'eyes' in the desert he knew so well *(Numbers 10:31)*. In turn, his descendants merited permanent residence in the Land of Israel *(Numbers 24:21-12)* and a place of honor among the Israelites forever. *(Samuel I, 15:5-6, Jeremiah 35:1-11)*

This value, too, is learned through the negative example of the Moabites and Ammonites. The verse quoted just above *(Deut 23:5)* continues *"...and because they hired against thee Balaam the son of Beor from Pethor of Aram-Naharaim, to curse thee."* Even beyond basic hospitality, the bread and water they were expected to bring would be a token of their blessing of the Israelite nation. Not only did they not bless the Israelites, but they even hired the wicked prophet to curse them. In turn, they themselves became cursed, according to *HaShem's* blessing to Abraham *(Genesis 12:3): "And I will bless them that bless thee, and I will curse him that curses you..."*

Any objective study of history will prove this to have been the case. Every empire or tyrant who rose to destroy or persecute the Jews met a miserable fate.

It is the unspoken duty of Noahides to aid, support and strengthen HaShem's designated nation of priests. Despite their human faults and weaknesses, the People of Israel remain the torch-bearers of Torah from generation to generation. Moreover, for reasons only fully known to *HaShem*, the Author of history so arranged that this one nation would be a great source of blessing to the others — *with no intention or conscious effort on their part.* It is simply the fulfillment of the second part of the above verse: *"...and through you shall all the families of the earth be blessed."*

In fact, it is clearly Divine Will that, no matter how much the Jewish People tries to assimilate and blend in to their host nations — *even against their will* — they are made to stand out, that the world might learn from the Divine message they bear. It is a phenomenon, which is fulfilled even through secular and secret Jews.

One who questions this phenomenon should consider the information below.

the Blessings of Law and Morality

Consider the treatment of women, the mass murder of captives for human sacrifice, and the accepted place of murder, rape and thievery in idolatrous societies to this day. In the ancient world, the masses of humanity reeled under the thumb of megalomaniacal "god-kings." Understand the revolution created by the Torah's teachings that all mankind is created in *HaShem's* image, and there being universal Divine Laws to which all are obligated — kings and commoners alike. However selective, hypocritical and impotent the world's moral compass proves to be; these ideas have had a profound influence over the last two thousand years. *What moral consciousness would there be today to speak of, without the teachings of the Written and Oral Torah — however altered and watered-down?*

Blessings to Human Health and the Environment

Putting aside the influence of Jewish medical knowledge on the development of medicine, consider Israel's mark on human health today:

How would the arid nations of the African Sahara be able to feed their populations without the precious Israeli know-how in desert agriculture they have employed over the last 50 years? Today these blessings have reached far beyond Africa, into Greece, the Dominican Republic, Egypt, South Africa, Mexico, Ecuador, Azerbaijan, Uzbekistan, Turkmenistan, India, China, Tibet, Russia, Turkey, Romania, the Philippines, and even Moslem countries that do not recognize Israel; namely Afghanistan, the United Arab Emirates, Indonesia, and Tunisia. (8)

In a world with increasing demands on the world's limited fresh water resources, what will be the ultimate value of Israel's breakthroughs and leadership in water-management technology? (9)

Also imagine a world still reeling from the scourge of polio, had Jonas Salk never invented the vaccine that would eradicate the disease from most of the countries of the world. (10) Consider Israel's experienced medical teams, trauma units and disaster aid missions, which are extended even to unfriendly nations struck by earthquakes, tsunamis, and uncontrollable wildfires. (11) (12) After the devastating earthquake that hit Haiti in 2010, where would over a thousand Hatians saved by Israel be, were it not for the state-of-the-art army field hospital that Israel set up there in record time?

Blessings to the U.S. Economy

Could the United States have been born without Haym Solomon, the most important financier of the American Revolution? (13)

Most recently, the dollar suffered a precipitous fall in value in 5768 (2008-9). When the Bank of Israel began purchasing 100 million dollars a day, halting the dollar's freefall, how many American firms and households were saved? (14)

In the face of increasing energy demands, the Israeli technology firm *Solel* has already reduced U.S. dependence on foreign oil by millions of barrels. This reduction will greatly increase with the completion of *Solel*'s construction of the world's largest solar power plant in the Mojave Desert. (15) Israel's revolutionary technology in solar power, water purification, and agriculture, and veritable army of brilliant software developers for Intel and other giant American corporations improve American lives at home.

Finally, the state of Israel serves as a free base for the U.S. military, a service that normally costs billions of dollars in other countries. This is no small contribution to a country wallowing in growing a national debt measuring in the trillions.

Blessings of Security

Israel's incredible military ingenuity – including UAVs, fighter jet servicing, know-how in counter-terrorist urban warfare, and more – is a gift that has saved and continues to save an uncounted number of American lives in the field of war.

Besides its technology, another key factor in the success of any military is the well-being and morale of its corps. What would life be like in the U.S. Navy, were it not for Commodore Uriah Phillips Levy, who abolished the Navy's policy of flogging? (16)

On the homefront, consider the effect of Islamic terror on daily life in Western countries today. Non-Jews dare not forget the words repeated by extremist Moslems themselves: "It's "the 'Saturday People' (the Jews) first, and the 'Sunday People' (the Christians) next." From the bombing of Iraq and Syria's nuclear reactors to the containment of Hizbullah (whose jihad-tentacles have even reached American soil); the state of Israel has fought that terror in its center of origin – *the Middle East* – for 62 years. Had there been no state of Israel in its thankless role as the West's first line of defense, how daunting a challenge would the Western militaries face on the field today, and what would daily life be like in Western countries today?

According to a most recent report, Israel's blessings to the nations are found today on the high seas. Israeli security agents are being hired by foreign shipping companies and cruise lines to help them face the menace of modern piracy. Today's sophisticated pirates, equipped with RPG rocket launchers, have made the sea off the coast of the Horn of Africa, West Africa off Nigeria, and the Malacca Straits in Southeast Asia the most dangerous shipping lanes in the world. Israeli security personnel are in high demand due to their experience, reputation and military training. (17)

Blessings of Civil Rights

The American Jews were the backbone of the African-American Civil Rights Movement, supporting the movement more than any other white group. Jews made up half of the white northern volunteers involved in the 1964 Mississippi Freedom Summer project, and half of the civil rights attorneys active in the South during the 1960's. While even the lay Jewish public (including my own parents) marched arm in arm with blacks through the streets, Jewish leaders were arrested with Rev. Dr. Martin Luther King, Jr. What would be the state of racial equality in America today — were it not for her Jews? (18)

This created the very social climate in which America could elect its first black president. Sadly, it does not appear that this fact in any way affects his harsh policies towards the ancestral homeland of the very people who made his election possible, and his administration viable.

These few examples hardly do justice; a more complete treatment of the subject could fill a set of books.

"To All the Families of the Earth" Through History

While I focused until now on Jewish blessings in the West, their blessed influence was no less great in the East. From the development of language, learning, and the spread of the martial arts; they had profound influence on the ancient cultures of China and Japan, and served the kings of Persia, India and Mongolia as loyal subjects and warriors. (19) In central Asia, the Jewish Khazar Empire influenced the Rus to give up their pillaging for permanent settlement, promoted and ensured the flow of trade between Eastern Europe and Asia, and was instrumental in containing the northern expansion of Islam. (19)

From the ancient tribes that settled the British Isles, to the well-known role that Jews played in the vitality of the economies of European monarchs. Jews were consistently a vehicle of blessing *in the very lands where they were most persistently persecuted.* What would Europe's age of exploration be without Jewish maps? Dr. Avigdor Shachan explains:

> Maps dating back to the most ancient era were owned by 15th century Jewish cartographers, notably Abraham Zacuto. The maps of this Jewish scholar are amazingly accurate and reliable. They served Christopher Columbus on his voyages. Spanish and Portuguese adventurers of that period used them on their voyages to discover the American continent. (20)

What is much less known is Jewish influence in the heart of Africa. The Igbo nation in Nigeria, with its vibrant Jewish heritage, are living testimony. (21) Even across the Atlantic, Catholic missionaries recorded ancient Jewish legends in the mouths of the old men of the Yucatan peninsula. (22) From the Maoris of New Zealand to the Yuchis (23) and Cherokees of native America (24), there is hardly an ancient culture on earth without profound evidence of direct or indirect Hebrew influence.

An encyclopedia could be written in an attempt to completely list and explain the blessings and benefits of the Jewish people to humanity. *Again, when one considers that there was no conscious, concerted Jewish effort in these matters over the millennia, HaShem's hand becomes even more apparent.* When the world comes to understand this principle, then the prophecy may be fulfilled:

> For then will I turn the peoples to a pure language, that they may all call upon the Name of

HaShem, to serve Him with one consent. *(Zephaniah 3:9)*

The Value Of Working For One's Sustenance And Well-Being

For Mental Well-Being and As a Safeguard Against Poverty

The ancient sages of Israel Shema`yah and Avtalion taught: "Love labor and hate lordship." *(Mishnah Avoth 1:10)* Labor is a value in and of itself, as much for Noahides as for Jews, since, as the Talmud teaches in *Kethuboth* 59b, *prolonged idleness can cause the mind to atrophy.* In *Pirkei Avos: Ethics of the Fathers*, there is a quote from a teaching of the late Rabbi Yisrael Salanter, explaining that people almost never die from hunger; instead they die due to prestige:

> They say: "This occupation is not prestigious enough for me; this one does not befit a person of my station." By contrast, the Talmud suggests: Skin carcasses in the marketplace and support yourself with the pay, and do not say, "I am a Kohen" or "I am a great man [and therefore I cannot do this lowly work]" *(Pesachim [sic] 113a).* Love work, teaches Shemayah *[sic]* — any type of work. (25)

Prestige also translates into overspending. Even the most meager income can make do when one frees himself from the trappings of popular Western culture — namely, expensive eating habits and entertainment. Many large, middle class families in Israel raise five to ten children in small apartments of only three or four rooms. This is a critical, timeless message for the world at large during this current global economic downturn, which is leaving so many out of work.

Working to Safeguard Family Happiness, Spiritual and Physical Well-Being

Idleness, even among those with no lack of money, is a poison that destroys families from within. In the non-Jewish world, this pearl of wisdom is summed up in the saying, "an idle mind is the devil's workshop." For Jews, it is legislated law that even if there is no lack of money and servants to do all labor, a woman may not sit idly without an occupation. Rather, she must do some form of labor at least for a portion of the day, for idleness leads to lewdness. *(Book of Women, Laws of Marriage 21:2)*

While the law remains what it is; in our world, this principle applies at least as much to men as to women. Addicted to the games and treacherous moral pitfalls of the internet, the armchair surfer — imagining he is free of the need for physical labor — lives in a virtual world that is so thrilling and mind-consuming that it replaces his need for natural human relationships. Above all, this post-modern form of idleness has generated a host of health problems associated with lack of exercise.

Mankind Was Created to Labor

Where in Torah is this value taught to humanity as a whole? *It is the very stated purpose for man's creation.* At first, HaShem describes the state of the world before man was formed:

> No shrub of the field was yet in the earth, and no herb of the field had yet sprung up; for HaShem God had not caused it to rain upon the earth, *and there was not a man to till the ground. (Genesis 2:5)*

HaShem then forms man of the dust of the earth, and places him in the garden of Eden *"to cultivate it and to steward it."*

(2:15) Later when man transgresses and is banished from the Garden, it is written: "Therefore *HaShem* God sent him forth from the garden of Eden, *to till the ground from where he was taken." (3:23)*

Whether he lived in an Edenic world or one overgrown with thorns and thistles, the natural state of man is to be occupied in some form of labor – especially agriculture. *Both his body and soul require it.*

Preserving The Earth And Its Species

Adam As Caretaker of the Earth

The very first mention of man's role in Creation (specifically in the Garden of Eden) is that he "cultivate it and guard [or 'steward' in this case] it" *(*in Hebrew *"le-`ovdah ul'shomrah", Genesis 2:15).* In fact, according to Oral Tradition, man –as caretaker of *HaShem's* world — was not initially permitted to slaughter meat for food until the Covenant with Noah, after the Flood. (26)

Applying the Torah Principle Today

Clearly, preservation of the earth is a basic Torah value for all humanity. While the wanton destruction of fruit trees is a prohibition to Jews from the Torah *(Deut. 20:19)*, it is also rabbinically forbidden for Jews to destroy or waste food, or to destroy useful objects *or a natural resource such as a spring. (Laws of Kings & Wars 6:14[10])*

Today, we are more keenly aware of the importance of natural resources to mankind, and how the dumping and improper burial of hazardous wastes can have life-threatening consequences. Moreover, they threaten the oceans, which sustain the world's supply of fish. The burning of coal causes the contamination of water resources for thousands of miles, and even around the globe. The systematic destruction of a large rainforest in one part of world adversely affects every human environment around the world. Today we are aware of the direct benefits to mankind of rainforest species that are being rapidly wiped out. Those benefits include medical treatment of critical illness (with no other known treatment), and superior textiles. Such forests are also home to thousands of indigenous people who depend on the forest for their livelihood.

The lack of an "explicit prohibition" against poisoning and ruining the earth's air, soil and water should be no consolation to the perpetrators. HaShem-fearing people must realize that this unbridled destruction is not only damaging to our quality of life, but an insult to the Creator, who — as stated above — placed man in the Garden of Eden to *cultivate and steward His handiwork.*

Sadly, these facts are manipulated by political and religious groups to serve different agendas. Rallying around the fear of "global warming", which is based on the shaky tenet of a "normal global temperature"; industries have been disrupted, resulting in an untold loss of jobs. A long dormant idolatry has been resurrected — a neo-paganism in the form of a cultish global reverence for "mother earth." *Those faithful to Torah should not be dismayed or deterred by these spiritual trends, but rather should do what is right because it is right — reducing pollution, recycling waste, and conserving resources.*

Sensitivity to Living Creatures

Without going to the Godless extreme of 'animal rights' activists, the value of sensitivity to animals for Noahides can be learned from the prophetic incident involving Balaam and his donkey *(Numbers 22:21-34)*. After Balaam repeatedly beats his donkey (who alone could see the angel with a drawn sword), Balaam's eyes are finally 'opened', and the terrifying angel berates the gentile prophet:

> And the angel of *HaShem* said to him: 'Why have you beaten your ass these three times? Behold, I have come forth as an adversary, because you have gone against me. And the ass saw me, and turned aside before me these three times; unless she had turned aside from me, surely now I would have slain you, and preserved her life. *(Numbers 22:32-33)*

The Torah value of respect for animal life can also be learned from the Commandments for Jews, such as the Commandment to shoo away the mother bird before taking its eggs *(Deut. 22:6-7)*, or the Commandment that Levites leave open spaces with specific measurements around their cities to accommodate their animals *(Numbers 35:1-5)*, the prohibition of preventing an animal from eating while it works *(Deut. 25:4 cf. Book of Judgments, Laws of Hiring 13:2)* and the various exceptions to rabbinical legislation that could cause suffering to animals carrying a burden *(Laws of the Sabbath 21:9-10, 25:25[27])*.

Note, in the Torah's narration of the story of Joseph, the repeated emphasis on the welfare the brothers' donkeys. When the brothers expressed their fear that they would be taken captive as slaves, they show concern for their donkeys as well. *(Gen.43:18)* When the brothers were shown hospitality at Joseph's palace, the Torah does not fail to mention that the donkeys were fed as well. *(43:24)* Finally, when the brothers were released in the morning, their donkeys' release is mentioned as well. *(44:3)*. Why would *HaShem* report such "trivia" in His Torah?

Note that these teachings do not constitute Torah recognition of any inherent 'rights' of animals. RaMBaM makes this perfectly clear. *(Laws of Prayer 9:7)* That would be inconsistent with other Torah teachings, such as the permission to freely slaughter meat for food, and *HaShem*'s special command to Joshua that he hamstring the horses he captured from the Canaanite armies *(Joshua 11:6)*. Rather, *the focus is on building our character* and on recognizing animals' utility for man. The Talmud teaches that *HaShem* gave us these Commandments (such as to shoo away the mother bird) in order to train us in the ways of kindness even towards animals, so that it might influence our character — particularly our behavior towards other people. *While these values are not conditions of the Noahide Covenant, the moral message should be clear.*

Understanding Abraham's Prayer

Many people believe that Abraham *(when he was called "Avram")* prayed on behalf of Sodom and Gomorrah, that the wicked would be spared on behalf of the righteous among them. This may be a prejudiced view rooted in today's liberal, Western values. A careful reading of the patriarch's prayer reveals that the focus of his prayer was *the place*. At the very first mention of Sodom and Gomorrah *(Genesis 13:10)*, the Torah describes its beauty, comparing it to the Garden of Eden. He prayed that this beautiful region be spared *HaShem*'s wrath in the merit of the righteous. (1)

The Flood As An Act of Earth-Preservation

To fully understand *HaShem*'s care for His creation, the earth, one must understand what actually triggered the great Flood of Noah. The Torah teaches the following:

> And *the earth was devastated [wa-tishahheth]* before God, and the earth was filled with violence. And *God saw the earth, and, behold, it was devastated [nish'hhathah]*; for all flesh had corrupted its way upon the earth. And God said unto Noah: 'The end of all flesh has come before Me; for the earth is filled with violence through them; and behold, *I will destroy*

them *[mash'hhitham]* with the earth.' *(Genesis 6:11-13)*

The common translation of Genesis 6:11 is, *"and the earth was corrupted before God."* If that were indeed the simple understanding of the Hebrew word, *wa-tishahheth*, that would mean that *HaShem* intended to *"corrupt them with the earth"*, God forbid! Clearly the meaning is that *HaShem* would *"destroy them with the earth"*, not *"to corrupt."* The root of these words is *shahhath*, meaning "destruction" or "devastation." The earth was not only corrupt from sin; *"the earth was devastated before God."*

Today there is considerable historical evidence of wars with weapons of mass destruction in the pre-flood world, both in ancient literature and confirmed, well-known physical areas of devastation on the earth: massive, circular fields of vitrified desert sand (transformed into glass by brief, searing heat), existing from antiquity. (27) The best example of this is Libyan desert glass of the Sahara desert, showing the same properties — the same silica fusion — as the sand at nuclear test sites. These desert sites defy scientific explanation *(as perhaps the very existence of some of those deserts)*, their being no sign of an impact crater that would suggest an asteroid culprit. Even microwave probes deep into the sand by satellite radar have come up empty-handed. (28) This suggests an altogether different explanation — a context for those chilling words in Genesis. *The very earth seems to declare the sinful devastation man wrought, the destruction bitterly lamented in the Torah.*

There is no intention on my part to discount the more traditional rabbinical understanding of *"shahhath"* as "corruption." The Torah lends itself to interpretation on different levels, and this has an important lesson to teach as well. However, as explained above, *"shahhath" as "corruption" cannot be the simple understanding of the text.*

Similarly, *"hhamas"* is commonly translated here as "robbery." Again, this interpretation carries an important lesson and I do not discredit it. However, it is not the simple meaning of the text. *In every other place in the Bible, 'hhamas' refers to some form of violence.* For example, in the book of Judges *(9:24)*, HaShem causes the inhabitants of Shechem to rebel against the rule of Abimelech, who had murdered his 70 brothers — the sons of Gideon, who was called Jerubaal. The text gives the reason HaShem stirred up the people against the warlord: *"so that the 'hhamas' against the seventy sons of Jerubaal would come back upon — and their blood would be placed upon — Abimelech their brother."* The hhamas spoken of here is clearly not robbery, but *violent murder.*

Now the meaning of the verses from the Torah account of Noah becomes clear.

The earth was being devastated through "hhamas" — human violence. The result, "the end of all flesh" by human design, was not far off. It was in order *to save* the righteous remnant of humanity, the earth and its creatures that *HaShem pre-empted* man and destroyed the world, as the verse concludes: *"...and behold, I will destroy them with the earth."*

The above teaching must be taken as an ominous warning to us in our times. The Book of Daniel foretells about a globe-girdling civilization that "will devour the entire earth, and crush and crumble it." (7:23) It also foretells the fate of that civilization: the entire "beast" is slated to be destroyed by fire. (7:11) When man begins to wantonly destroy the earth and its creatures, HaShem responds measure for measure, pre-empting man in order to save the earth with its righteous remnant.

Conclusion, a New Book to Come

To fully understand this warning, one must understand:

- the precise meaning of prophecies in the Book of Daniel (in light of those in Ezekiel and Zechariah)

- the ancient visions of Adam and Seth and the monument built by Shem that still remains, to warn future generations of a *mabbul esh* — a destruction through fire.

- The precise time figures concealed in Daniel's cryptic verses.

This and more is the included in my coming book, *Song of the Creator* (© All Rights Reserved) may it be completed soon and according to *HaShem*'s Will, with His blessing.

But on a more basic level, one must first know what HaShem has expected and continues to expect of mankind since the beginning, which I hope this first book helps to clarify. Whatever befalls mankind, knowing how to build a world according to *HaShem*'s Will, will undoubtedly give us the faith and strength to persevere.

However bleak our reality may appear, the Torah gives an optimistic view of the world and its destiny. The belief in the coming of the true messiah-king and the era he will usher in, is a cardinal tenet of faith for the Jew. This vision is grounded in reality. There is strong evidence that – despite the horrors of the last century and our heightened awareness of acts of violence around the globe – in the larger context of history, humanity's violence is actually decreasing. (29)

May the day arrive soon that in all spheres — between man and *HaShem*, between man and man, and even between man and himself — the words of the prophet will be fulfilled:

They shall not hurt nor destroy in all My holy mountain; for the earth shall be full of the knowledge of *HaShem*, as the waters cover the sea." *(Isaiah 9:10)*

NOTES

(1) The insights into Avram's failure to assume authority over the land, and Avram's prayer for Sodom and Gomorrah are teachings of Nathanel `Ozeri, of blessed memory. "Nati", as he is fondly remembered, a beloved teacher and pioneer from the hills of Hevron, was murdered in cold blood by Arabs in 5762 (2002) at age of 34. He was a devoted husband and father, as well as a dedicated and brilliant Torah scholar — a knowledgeable and stalwart student of RaMBaM, no less. Moreover, he was a valiant man of action. A remarkable teacher of agriculture and raising farm animals to the residents of Judah and Samaria, he was a popular leader and fearless example to the settlers of the hill country of the Land of Israel. May his blood be avenged.

(2) *Elohim* is not only a holy name of God in Hebrew, but "senior judge." *HaShem* has no image or form. Rather, He created a unique being who — like Him — would possess the faculty of judgment. The verse could therefore be rendered, "And God created the human in His own likeness, in the likeness of **a judge** He created him..." *(1:27)*

(3) Item found at: *The Dennis Prager Store:* GENESIS I Chapters 1-6, found at: http://stores.dennisprager.com/

(4) Owen, James, "Homosexual Activity Among Animals Stirs Debate," July 23, 2004. A web-article at:
news.nationalgeographic.com/news/2004/07/0722_040722_gayanimal.html

(5) De Waal, Franz B.M., "Bonobo Sex and Society" (Originally published in the March 1995 issue of *SCIENTIFIC AMERICAN,* pp. 82-88). A web-article found at: *songweaver.com/info/bonobos.html*

(6) According to Mori Shelomo ben Avraham, this is a typical syntactical shortened structure to say in this case, "'let us go to the field' and they did so." That is to say, "what he said is

129

that they did." Compare to *Genesis 42:25, I Samuel 9:27, Nehemiah 13:19,* and *Jonah 2:11.* Most translators and commentators do not get this fine syntactic point.

(7) In the 2nd definition of "violence" in Webster's Ninth New Collegiate Dictionary, "outrage" is given as a synonym. (*Webster's Ninth New Collegiate Dictionary.* Merriam Webster Inc., 1986. 1563 pp.)

(8) Hazan, Jenny, "Israel Agricultural Know-How Helps The Developing World Bloom," October 09, 2006. A web-article at *Israel21c.*org, found at: *www.israel21c.org*

— *See Also:*
"Israeli Delegation Addresses UN Commission On Sustainable Development," February 27, 2009. A web-article at Israel Ministry of Foreign Affairs, found at: *www.mfa.gov.il*

"Israeli Agricultural Expertise Aids Tibetan Refugees", May 26, 2007. A web-article at The Israel Export & International Cooperation Institute: Agrotechnology, found at: *www.export.gov.il/Eng/Articles*

(9) Sandler, Neal, Israel, "Waterworks for the World?" December 30, 2005. A web-article at BusinessWeek.com: *businessweek.com/technology/content/dec2005/tc20051230 _495029.htm*

(10) Entry for "Polio Vaccine" at *Wikipedia: The Free Encyclopedia,* found at: *en.wikipedia.org/wiki/Polio_vaccine*

(11) Entry for "ZAKA" at *Wikipedia: The Free Encyclopedia,* found at: *en.wikipedia.org/wiki/ZAKA_*

(12) "Israeli Humanitarian Relief — MASHAV — the Israel Foreign Ministry Center for International Cooperation," October 1, 2002. A web-article at *Israel Ministry of Foreign Affairs,* found at:
mfa.gov.il/MFA/Mashav_International Development/Activities

(13) Entry for "Haym Solomon," *Wikipedia: The Free Encyclopedia*, found at: *en.wikipedia.org/wiki/ Haym_Solomon*

(14) Maoz, Yuval and Sheva, Nathan, "Dollar jumps 4% as Israel Bank Announces Plan to Buy $100M a Day," appearing July 10, 2008. A web-article at *www.haaretz.com*

(15) Israel21c staff, "Israel's Solel to build largest solar park in world in California," July 26, 2007. A web-article at Israel21c, found at: *www.israel21c.org*

(16) Entry for "Uriah P. Levy" at *Wikipedia: The Free Encyclopedia*, found at: *en.wikipedia.org/wiki/ Uriah_P._Levy*

(17) Koosterman, Karin, "Shiver Me Timbers, Israelis Are Fighting Pirates At Sea," May 28, 2009. A web-article at *www.israel21c.org*

(18) Entry for "African-American Civil Rights Movement (1955-1968)" at *Wikipedia: The Free Encyclopedia*, found at: *en.wikipedia.org/wiki/American_Civil_Rights_Movement(1955-1968)*

(19) Brook, Kevin Alan, *The Jews of Khazaria,* Jason Aronson Inc., New Jersey 1999. 352 pp.

(20) Shachan, Dr. Avigdor, *In the Footsteps of the Lost Ten Tribes* (Translated from the Hebrew), Devorah Publishing Company, USA 2007. 452 pp.

(21) See the *Igbo Israel Online* website at*: igboisrael.com.*

(22) Velikovsky, Immanuel, *Ages in Chaos*, Buccaneer Books, New York 1950. 401 pp.

(23) Gordon, Cyrus, *Before Columbus: Links Between the Old World and Ancient America*, Crown Publishers Inc., New York 1971. 224 pp.

(24) One of the most significant evidence of the Jewish-Cherokee link is found in the following ethnographic work done over 200 years ago:

Adair, James, *The History of the American Indians, Particularly Those Nations Adjoining to the Mississippi East and West Florida, Georgia, South and North Carolina, and Virginia*, Printed for E. and C. Dilly, London 1775. Online version edited by John Mark Ockerbloom at *The Online Books Page*, found at: onlinebooks.library.upenn.edu /webbin/book/lookupid?key=olbp10190

(25) Lieber, Rabbi Moshe, *The Pirkei Avos Ethics of the Fathers Treasury*, Mesorah Publications Ltd, Brooklyn NY 1995. 439 pp.

(26) See *Laws of Kings and Wars 9:1-2(1)*. According to Oral tradition, non-ritual slaughtering of animals for meat (except as *qorban*-offerings) was only permitted after the *HaShem*'s Covenant with Noah. In the aftermath of the rampant bestiality in the pre-Flood world, permitting man to slaughter for meat would give man a more tangible awareness as to the distinction between human and beast. Furthermore, by saving the world's creatures from extinction, the new progenitors of humanity had earned the right to slaughter them for meat — albeit in a responsible way.

(27) Noorbergen, Rene, *Secrets of the Lost Races: New Discoveries of Advanced Technology in Ancient Civilizations*. Teach Services Publishing, June 2001. 230 pp.

(28) A number of web sources exist on this subject. Although critical thinking and examination of the sources is required to distinguish between fact and interpretation; to this author's understanding, the hard evidence stands for itself. More significantly, it supports the Torah's account according to its simple, direct meaning:

- Corliss, William R., "Flotsam On the Great Sand Sea." A web-article at *Science Frontiers Online* No. 126: Nov-Dec. 1999. © 1999-2000: sciencefrontiers.com/sf126 /sf126p06.htm

- Childress, David Hatcher, "The Evidence For Ancient Atomic Warfare," *Nexus Magazine* Vol. 7, No. 6: Aug-Sept

2000. *bibliotecapleyades.net/ancientatomicwar* (see report by Albion W. Hart quoted from Steiger, Brad and Ron Calais, Mysteries of Time & Space, Prentice Hall, New Jersey, 1974.)

- Entry for 'Lybian Desert Glass', at *Wikipedia: The Free Encyclopedia*: *en.wikipedia.org/wiki/Libyan_desert_glass*

- Steiger, Brad, "Numerous evidence of Pre-Historic Nuclear War exists: Columns of Smoke Rose as if from a Mighty Furnace" © 2007, Brad Steiger. A web-article at My News — Marc Jäger: *marcjager.com/green-glass.html*

(29) Although this article – written by a secular Jew – includes a disgraceful jab at the Torah, revealing his ignorance; the objective evidence he brings on the progress of humanity do seem correct:

Pinker, Steven, "A History of Violence" (First published in *The New Republic* March 17, 2007). A web-article at *www.edge.org/3rd_culture/pinker07*

PART IV

FREQUENTLY ASKED QUESTIONS

Answers to common questions about
the challenges of living according to
HaShem's Code of Law in our times

נָטִיתִי לִבִּי לַעֲשׂוֹת חֻקֶּיךָ, לְעוֹלָם עֵקֶב.

(תהילים קיט,קיב)

*I have inclined my heart
to perform Your statutes,
forever at every step.*

(Psalms 119,112)

Interacting With Non-Noahides

1) As a new Noahide, how do I explain my life-changing choice to my non-Noahide family and friends?

First of all, offering unsolicited explanations of your beliefs is generally unwise, except in the following cases: (a) to defend your beliefs, actions, and way of life against those who put them down in front of others, (b) to explain your different behavior (such as why you might choose not to attend the baptism of a friend's newborn child) in order to prevent insult, or (c) to attract open-minded individuals who could be positively influenced by your choice.

However, beyond those situations, new acquaintances may ask, and it is important to know what to answer. Here are a few guiding principles:

- There is no need or necessary benefit in accentuating your differences, as if living as a Noahide were something odd. Sometimes it is easier to influence your peers by showing how "normal" it is to be a Noahide.

- Try not, especially at first, to put down other individuals or their beliefs in order to prove the correct path (unless you know for certain the person shares those negative views). It is nearly always more powerful and effective to emphasize what you find positive, correct, and beautiful in authentic Torah.

- Honesty and simplicity are generally the best policy. To share your own experiences and evolution of thought is generally far more effective than trying to deliver someone else's arguments or experiences that happen to inspire you. However, if that is what inspired you to keep the Torah, share those ideas and tell where you learned them. Your humble recommendation may attract the person to the same flame of Torah that kindled your own.

- BOOKS: You may want to recommend books that offer proof and a rational basis for authentic Torah tradition, or expose the lies and deception of Christianity – such as the materials of Outreach Judaism by Rabbi Tovia Singer. Only if the person's interest has been kindled and they desire to learn the details of Noahide observance would I recommend *Guide for the Noahide*.

    That being said, Noahide friends have told me that there is no better book sells the truth more than the Bible itself. To honest readers who have left Jesus, it generally proves itself. However, many an honest reader will find difficulty with the concept of an Oral Law. To help such people – Jew and Noahide – I recommend a soon-to-be published book of mine, *Eighteen Proofs of the Authenticity of the Oral Tradition*.

- Be certain to listen to the other person. Listening will help you to understand his mentality, where he is spiritually and intellectually, and what he may be wrestling with. This will aid you immensely in your communication, and make the person feel he isn't being preached to. For that, it is good to ask the person questions such as: "what do you think about __?", "what do you believe about __?", or "is it only me, or do you also have questions about / a problem with __?"

- Finally, don't speak too much. Leave the other person thirsting for more, rather than saturated with more well-meaning information than he can digest.

2) **As a new Noahide, how do I relate to idolaters among my family and friends?**

First of all, unlike in Christianity, there is no mention in the Noahide Covenant – even in the accompanying rabbinical laws – of any obligation for a Noahide to go out and "save" one's family and peers.

That should make a Noahide far more tolerant and respectable in the eyes of his peers than someone who joined some cult, *HaShem*-forbid.

Unlike for the Jew, short of committing idolatry and adultery, there are no laws limiting a Noahide's social interaction with idolaters. However, it is *a fact of human nature* that we are influenced by the beliefs and actions of our peers; hence the obligation for Jews to attach themselves to Torah scholars, and the prohibition for Jews to befriend the wicked. *(Book of Knowledge, Laws of Personal Dispositions 6:1-2)* Noahides are greatly encouraged to associate with righteous Noahides and Jews in every way possible (not only socially, but in business as well), and to restrict one's association with idolaters to a minimum. Again, however, this is a value – not a law.

3) **Can I go to religious events of Christian or Hindu family, such as weddings and funerals? Can I enter a church or idolatrous temple for such a function?**

Unlike for Jews, there is no prohibition for Noahides to attend such religious events, or entering places of idol worship. However, for the same reasons mentioned in the above response, it is wise to refrain whenever possible. It is the practice of an elder Noahide friend of mine to politely decline any invitation to any such function except a wedding or funeral. This balanced approach is praiseworthy.

4) **What do I do if idolaters give me a gift that is idolatrous in nature – such as statue of Buddha or an artistic depiction of an Aztec god, etc?**

Again, as opposed to *halakhah* (applied Torah law) for Jews, there is no prohibition for Noahides to own an idolatrous object such as a statue; only to serve it. However, even if a Noahide wishes to emulate Abraham and destroy idolatry to the degree he is able, there is generally nothing to be gained

– but much to be lost – by embarrassing the giver. Unless the gift was intended to degrade the Noahide's religious beliefs, the most one may want to do – if the giver is a friend – is to gently inform him in private that, while you truly appreciate the thought, the item is inappropriate, as you are a Noahide. Depending on the situation, the gift could present an opportunity to educate an open-minded friend or family member about the Seven Laws. However, while one may thus choose to sanctify God's Name, he need not feel legally compelled to flatly refuse the gift. It is left to one's individual judgment.

5) *If my spouse brings home an X-mas tree or insists on doing so, what should I do?*

After discussion with a former Baptist minister, it seems clear that the traditions surrounding the X-mas tree are **not** rites of idol worship. Neither is it an *Asherah* tree, a rabbinical prohibition to Noahides. Rather, the tree is a pagan custom that Christians adopted, becoming associated with their holiday. Accordingly, although a God-fearing Noahide should ordinarily flee from such customs, this is an area where a Noahide can be lenient on his loved ones if they are finding the move to Noahide observance too drastic and difficult.

6) *When I need to fill out an application for employment or otherwise, what should I, as a Noahide, put as my religion?*

Although it may raise eyebrows and require further explanation, if Noahide observance is to ever to enter the public consciousness and take root as a mainstream religious movement, Noahides must become confident and persistent enough to demand recognition. Depending on the circumstances, labeling themselves as a Noahides in applications could contribute to that end.

Frequently Asked Questions

However, in the military, one's religion defines the religious services that will be available to him or her. Since Noahide soldiers can generally do no better than be counseled by an Orthodox Jewish chaplain, it makes the most sense to describe one's faith as a form of Orthodox Judaism. This will entitle the Noahide soldier to be counseled by a chaplain who – if not a Torah scholar – is a basically Torah-observant individual trained to counsel others according to Orthodox Torah values.

7) How can a Noahide in military service or in prison get counseling?

Again, while there are those who believe Noahides should have their own chaplains, I see little need. Rather, Jewish chaplains need to become sensitized and trained to deal with the spiritual needs of Noahides. As Noahide scholar James D. Long aptly put it: "If non-military Noahides look to a rabbi for spiritual direction, why not a Noahide soldier?" At worst, if the chaplain is ignorant about the Noahide laws, this book can help educate and sensitize him to the obligations and needs of Noahides, and help him to fulfill his greater Israelite role as a "priest to the nations."

Ending The Loneliness, Getting Involved

8) A Noahide can feel so lonely not belonging to any of the recognized religions. Are there Noahide communities or internet groups I can join?

Unfortunately, there are currently very few places where there are groups of Noahides living in close proximity to one another. However, with access to the internet, there are a myriad of websites and resources (especially with social networking sites) available to the Noahide.

Here is a short list of a few notable online Torah sources for Noahides and Noahide discussions groups. Others exist that I do not list in interests of brevity, and others still others on

141

which I have no knowledge. There is no slight or insult intended towards those groups I do not mention.

Being that many of the Noahide groups are partly associated with and served by scholars whose views contradict the path of RaMBaM – the ancient, rational Torah tradition of Talmudic sages – my listing them here does not imply my approval of all the Torah content being taught there. Although there is much room for improvement in the quality of the Torah substance found on these sites; they represent vibrant, growing and decent online Noahide communities.

- **Mesora.org:** *(mesora.org/discussions)*
  Created and maintained by Jewish Torah scholars, this site includes an active discussion group open to Noahides. A wellspring of rational Torah, its articles are well-researched, and rooted in one of the most parallel Torah perspectives one can find to our own: that of serious students of RaMBaM.

- **Noahide Nations:** *(noahidenations.com)*
  Founded and moderated by Ray Petterson, this Noahide site has given the grassroots Noahide movement in the U.S. a strong media presence and active locus of Noahide learning. The "Noahide Nations" online forum is found at Yahoo Groups.

- **Noahide Yahoo List:** An older, even more active Noahide discussion group at Yahoo groups, moderated by Frances Makarova, is "Noahides."

- **Virtual Bnai Noah / Noahide Community:** This is an active Facebook community, from which one can find links to other online Noahide groups.

- **Lazer Beams:** This is a rich Hasidic website with a "B'nei Noach" blog rich with articles and discussion managed by Rabbi Lazer Brody. In light of the differences between the outlooks of RaMBaM and the Hasidic masters, some may wonder why I, a loyal student of RaMBaM, recommend this blog to Noahides — particularly to those in emotional distress and spiritual turmoil.

First, Rabbi Brody's focus is not *halakhah*, but healthy, spiritual psychology, and his teachings have touched the lives of multitudes in Israel and abroad, Jews and Noahides alike. One may draw precious emotional strength from this teacher, while remaining firmly rooted in *halakhah* according to RaMBaM. It could also be an easier place to start for friends and family members with an emotional block to the service of God through laws and ordinances, and may only be reached through a more spiritual approach.

Secondly, the key Breslover teachings he emphasizes are rooted in *Mishneh Torah*: Pure and personal prayer from the heart, *(Book of Love, Laws of Blessings 10:28[26])*, meditating in nature *(Book of Knowledge, Laws of Foundations of Torah 2:1, 4:19[12])*, the importance of joy and the dangers of depression and anger. *(Ibid. 7:8[4], Book of Women, Laws of Marriage 15:20 among many other sources)*

In fact, from within the context of the *halakhah*, RaMBaM directs the "spiritually ill" to the doctors of the soul – the sages of Israel. *(Book of Foundations of Torah, Laws of Personal Dispositions 1-4[1,2])* He describes how the rabbis direct their patients to the opposite extreme, in order to bring them back to the middle path. This is similar to a medical doctor who prescribes an altered diet from the norm to an ill patient.

In our world – an entire generation wallowing in grave spiritual illness from lack of *emunah* (faith in *HaShem*) – there is an important place for a spiritual counselor such as Rabbi Brody who inspires that faith. He is a veteran specialist with decades of experience in the field of family and emotional counseling. His simple practical teachings of how to overcome personal suffering, defeat anger and substance abuse, create peace in the home and even improve physical health through unencumbered faith and joy have literally saved lives. One need not identify as "Hasidic" to benefit from his wisdom.

- **The *Ohel Moshe* Society (Beth Midrash Ohel Moshe):** *(www.torathmoshe.com)* This site, our own website, includes a slowly growing Beth Midrash (Study Hall) section with the category "Torath B'nei NoaH (Torah for Noahides)." Our forum "Ohalmosha" (Beith Midrash Ohel Moshe) at Yahoo Groups, is open to Noahides who are serious about Torah observance, as it is to serious Jews.

9) How can I meet similar Noahide singles like myself?

For over a decade, the traditional places for Noahides to meet have been Torah classes and study groups for Noahides. From the above-mentioned web discussion groups, one can find out about any local classes for Noahides in one's area. While such physical classes can be few and sparse, there are yearly Noahide conventions, such as those organized by the Vendyl Jones Research Institute and Noahide Nations. These provide quality opportunities for getting to meet, learn Torah with, and become well-acquainted with new Noahide friends.

However, the simplest resource available to Noahide singles is the internet. There are a number of public forums and discussion groups for Noahide singles, although it is often difficult for people to feel free to socialize in such open

Frequently Asked Questions

forums online. *HaShem*-willing, the website *bnsingles.com* will be returning soon, and will provide a professional online matchmaking resource after the pattern of J-Date and other successful dating sites, including individual profiles and private chat rooms. It should be launched by no later than July 2010.

10) Can a Noahide pray in an Orthodox synagogue? How does one approach the local rabbi?

King Solomon built the Holy Temple to be a house of prayer for all nations. *(Isaiah 56:7)* It is only natural that Orthodox synagogues open their doors to Noahides as well. In general, a growing number of rabbis are kind and welcoming. However, it is not uncommon for rabbis to be less inviting. Before they are judged negatively, their perspective and concerns must be understood and respected.

Although Noahide guests are rarely more than a few, it is natural for a community rabbi who is unfamiliar with Noahides to fear a sudden influx of non-Jews into the synagogue – with whatever spiritual baggage they may be carrying from their past. He might be concerned at the prospect of attractive, religious Noahide singles mixing with the Jewish singles among his flock. This could be aggravated by the growing crisis in the Orthodox world of older Jewish singles who cannot find a mate. Synagogue services typically serve as one of the few ways for singles to meet. In short, he may see Noahides as a potential Trojan horse.

Even more likely, a community rabbi may simply feel unable to help Noahides due to his limited resources – the most precious of which being his time. Consider the constant, uphill battle that rabbis face just in taking care of their own.

The Orthodox rabbi typically devotes his whole self – his days and nights, in sickness and health — to preventing his flock from assimilation. He must create as pure a Torah atmosphere as possible for his Diaspora Jews, a good percentage of which are typically returnees to Torah observance, converts in training, and barely-observant families that he struggles to keep from drifting even further away. A dwindling budget due to the worsening economy makes community resources even harder to share beyond the needs of those with an actual Divine obligation to learn Torah and pray according to *halakhah*.

A Noahide must therefore understand when a typically overworked, underpaid rabbi answers his call with an irritated, "what do you want?" or a patronizing "how nice," etc. Rather than perceiving this as the tone of a narrow-minded hypocrite who doesn't understand the eternal role of the Jewish People; *take it as the guarded approach of a devoted, protective shepherd.*

In your initial ice-breaking conversation, be certain the rabbi understands from the outset that you are fully Torah-centered, and harbor no idolatrous beliefs. Your sole intention is to pray and learn Torah respectfully with his congregation. Unfortunately, Noahide law is not a subject studied by rabbis for their certification, and ignorance on the subject abounds. A good way to initiate dialogue with your local rabbi is to give or loan him this book, so that he can become familiar with the laws and issues.

I urge rabbis to seize the opportunity to sanctify *HaShem's* Name by reaching out to non-Jews in fulfillment of our role as a "kingdom of priests" whenever possible – particularly at this time, when the movement is still in its infancy, and friends of the Jewish People are becoming fewer.

Whatever spiritual baggage Noahides may have is likely to have a far less negative influence on a community than that of newly-observant Jews carried over from their past. Moreover, *the very presence of non-Jews at services and Torah classes is likely to inspire Jews to behave better than they ordinarily would amongst themselves.* If limited resources are a concern, Noahide donations for synagogues are permitted to be used. And if ever a large number of Noahides become regular attendees of synagogue services and intermingling becomes a concern, a special Noahide section could be created besides the traditional sections for Jewish men and women.

Torah Outlook

11) *I am fascinated by Talmud, Hasidism and kosher mysticism, so that I can understand Torah and God's Ways better. Should I, as a Noahide, learn such subjects?*

The answer to this question is found in Part II, Section B of this work. A broader introduction to the subject can be found in the Part I, *Where is the Spirituality?*

12) *Can one still remain a proper Noahide and still believe in Jesus as a prophet, or a great sage?*

A better question would be, is it forbidden for a Noahide to hold non-idolatrous beliefs that are foolish? The answer is no, such beliefs are not forbidden as such. So long as he does not espouse idolatrous beliefs regarding Jesus or commit idolatry *(including praying to him, even as a intermediary between himself and the Creator)*, there is no prohibition for a Noahide to foolishly believe in Jesus as a "prophet", "sage", or even "potential messiah", etc.

However, as followers of authentic rabbinical Torah who see the Torah scholars of Israel as their priesthood, it is *unseemly* for a Noahide to honor the memory of a man who, according to Talmudic legend, was a sorcerer and an idol-worshipper who caused the masses to sin. *(Babylonian Talmud 43a, M.T. Book of Knowledge, Laws of Idolatry 3:19[10])* From the very first book of the "New Testament", he is portrayed as a man who saw himself as a God who commanded the host of heaven and forgave sin himself. To anyone who has learned

Torah, to see such a Jew as observant to begin with is ridiculous.

How could a Noahide, of all people, honor the memory of a man remembered for his policy not to teach Torah to non-Jews? *(Matthew 10:5,6)* That is a minor slight indeed, compared to Mark 2:25-27, where Jesus verbally refers to non-Jews as dogs to their face – in this case a gentile woman who had traveled a great distance to beg of him to heal her daughter. (1) While healing an idolatress may not have been permitted under the circumstances, the Sages taught: "Do not be spiteful towards any person." *(Mishnah tractate Avoth 4:3)* Any rabbi worth his salt would consider such cruel words to a non-Jew a desecration of God's Name.

On the contrary, the Sages were known for teachings such as, *"We are obliged to feed the gentile poor [idolaters] in exactly the same manner as we feed the Jewish poor." (Ibid. tractate Gittin 61a)* This is rooted in a central Torah principle expressed in Psalm 145:9: "*HaShem* is good to all, and His love extends over all His works." Hardly an obscure verse, this very psalm is recited by Jews in our prayer liturgy three times daily. It is the Scriptural source for the rabbinical teaching that *one should not overwork non-Jewish servants, but treat them with kindness and mercy. (M.T. Laws of Slaves 9:13[8])*

Consider Jesus' restrictions on God's general love for those who observe His Commandments. He reportedly taught: "He who believes in the Son has everlasting life. But he who does not believe in the Son shall not see life, but shall suffer the everlasting wrath of God." *(John 3:5)* "I surely say to you: Unless a man is born of water and the Spirit [undergoes full conversion to his religion], he cannot enter the Kingdom of God." *(John 3:36)* In other words, if one does not believe in Jesus, one has no place in the World to Come (eternal life).

Contrast this with the authentic Oral Torah teaching: *"The righteous of all nations have a place in the World to Come." (Tosefta, tractate Sanhedrin 13)* Moreover, one Talmudic sage exclaimed:

> I bring heaven and earth to witness that *the Divine Spirit rests upon a non-Jew as well as upon a Jew*, upon a woman as well as upon a man, upon a maidservant as well as a manservant. All depends on the deeds of the particular individual. *(Yalqut Shim'oni, Judges 42, Chapter 4, from Midrash Tanhhumah)*

Again we see that the vindictive teachings attributed to Jesus are not those of a loyal Torah student, much less a Torah sage.

Here is a short background to the mark of true prophecy. According to *halakhah*, unlike a negative prophecy which might not occur (*HaShem* can always have mercy and nullify an evil decree *[see Joel 2:13, Jonah 4:2]*), any *good* vision of a future event spoken by a prophet *must* occur, and within the time-frame declared by the prophet. *(See Jeremiah 28:7-9 and II Kings 10:10 cf. Deut. 18:21)* If any detail of the prophecy is left unfulfilled, or the event does not occur in its declared time, the individual is proven to be a false prophet, and he is liable to the death penalty by stoning. *(Laws of Foundations of Torah ch.10)*

In Matthew 4:17, Jesus begins preaching, *"Repent ye, for the kingdom of heaven is at hand."* There is no escaping the plain meaning of this statement. Not only does Jesus allegedly prophesy here regarding the Kingdom of heaven – the long awaited Redemption – but he gives a time period. *Very soon.* That is why he and his followers urge everyone to make haste and repent before the coming time of Divine Judgment. This is befitting a man who not only wanted to be recognized as one who speaks the Word of God, but – according to

Christian teachings – the Jewish messiah. However, as history witnessed, nothing of Jesus' messianic prophecy occurred. If the words attributed to him are historically accurate, he appears to have been a false prophet.

Regarding Jesus' false messiahship, RaMBaM explains:

> Could there be a greater stumbling block than this: that all the prophets spoke of the messiah as a savior who would redeem Israel [from oppression], ingather their exiles and strengthen [the observance of] the Commandments – while this man brought about the destruction of Israel by the sword, that their remnant be scattered and degraded, and that the Torah be replaced, and the majority of the world to be mislead to serve a god besides *HaShem*?! *(Book of Judges, Laws of Kings and Wars 11:10)*

I can somewhat understand a regular uninformed non-Jew espousing he was a prophet or potential messiah, but a Noahide who studies and lives by the Oral traditions preserved by Israel from Moses at Mt. Sinai?!

Responding to Haters of Israel

13) *I received a nasty email by right-wing Christian anti-Semites who mock me for being a "stooge" for the Jewish people, while they don't even see me as even having a soul! I was taught that a Noahide has a place in the World to Come. What is the truth, and how do I answer such people?*

The fact that an observant Noahide indeed merits the Life of the World to Come has been mentioned and cited with its sources both in *Mishneh Torah* and Talmud. *(See Part II Section B-3)* Such people generally have a seething hate for the Jewish People, often based on verses from Talmud taken out of context that are widely disseminated on the internet. Some of their key arguments are dismantled in Part I: *Noahide Justice in Proper Perspective: Answering the Fearmongers and Anti-Semites*. As stated there, the best source I've seen publicly clearing the Talmud of such libel is the website of Rabbi Gil Student: "The Real Truth About the Talmud" *(talmud.faithweb.com)*. A Noahide would be wise to arm himself with the sources gathered and translated by the rabbi.

If the anti-Semite is a Christian, it may suffice to quote him *Zechariah 8:23*:

> Thus says *HaShem* of hosts: In those days it shall come to pass, that ten men from all the language-groups of the nations, shall take hold of the corner of the garment of a Jewish man, saying: "We will go with you, for we have heard that God is with you."

I would not let the conversation end before reminding him of what is taught in Matthew 23:2-3 in the name of Jesus himself:

> The scribes and Pharisees sit in the seat of Moses; *therefore all that they tell you, do and observe*, but do not according to their deeds; for they say things and do not do them.

I heard that there are those foolishly claim that "the seat of Moses" here refers to some special "seat" that featured in synagogues of the time; there was no intention here to put the Sages on a pedestal as fulfilling the leadership role of Moses. I would ask that they consider Jethro's words to Moses in Ex. 18:13-26, and the implementation of God's Command in Numbers 11:16-17. *The rabbinical judges literally take over a major part of Moses' daily role of judgment.* This is clearly the context of the words attributed to Jesus.

Furthermore, in the above text, Jesus is using the fact the Rabbis sit "in the seat of Moses" as the reason why – even if they are corrupt, God forbid – one must do all that they say. Why would the Rabbis have such authority simply by virtue of their sitting in a fancy seat in their synagogues?!

In his brilliant decoding of the classical Christian texts, Rabbi Tovia Singer employs the following method to derive from the Gospels what may, indeed, have been teachings of the true historical Jesus. If a verse attributed to Jesus appears to have escaped the censors' eyes – since it appears to teach *the opposite* of what the Church founders preached (an embarrassment to Christianity) – there is a chance it is historically accurate. *Can there be anything more embarrassing to the future Church than Jesus promoting the Pharisee Rabbis as "sitting in the seat of Moses", exhorting his followers to fulfill "all that they tell you"?!*

14) **How do I answer Moslems who ridicule me for attaching myself to a nation of "murderers" and "thieves", followers of the rabbis who "changed the Torah"?**

First, if the individual is open to an intelligent answer, I would make him realize how Islam, like Christianity, reveres a text that – unbeknownst to the simple masses – requires solid faith in the Oral Tradition of the *Perushim* (Pharisees, the Rabbis).

In Islam, Jesus is considered to be one of the true prophets of Allah: a true bearer of Allah's word in his time. Vicariously, the reverent Moslem must either accept the teaching of Jesus quoted above (that the Pharisaic Rabbis sit in the seat of Moses and all must do according to what they teach) or contradict his own religion. Therefore, even according to Islam, if one must heed the teachings of *Nebi 'Issa* ("prophet Jesus"), then *every Torah instruction of the "scribes and*

Frequently Asked Questions

Pharisees" must be obeyed. Again, since this verse undermines the Christian religion, Moslems can be certain that this verse is no corruption or later addition to the historical words of their *Nebi 'Issa*.

I would then proceed to prove this truth from passages in their own Qur'an. (2)

First, to refute the lie that the nation of Israel stole another people's land, I would quote their own prophet who taught that the land of Israel was given to the People of Moses by Allah, as it is written:

> Bear in mind the words of Moses to his People [Children of Israel]. He said: "Remember, my People, the favor which God has bestowed upon you. He has raised up prophets among you, made you kings (Kingdom of David and Solomon and the Davidic Dynasty), and has given you that which He has given to no other nation [the Written and Oral *Torah* and the Land of Israel]. *Enter, my People, the holy land* [Land of Israel] *which God has assigned for you. Do not turn back, and thus lose all.*" [*Qur'an, The Table, Sura 5:20*]

This is according to Allah's special favor for the Jews, as it is written:

> "Children of Israel, remember the favor I [*Allah*] have bestowed upon you, and that I exalted you above the nations." [*Qur'an, The Cow, Sura 2:47*]

I would note how the People of Moses has clearly *retained* Allah's favor, as He has blessed Israel with victory over so many Moslem foes, time and again. Israel's long exile, Allah's enduring favor, and Israel's eventual return to their Allah-given land were clearly prophesied by Moses – a true prophet in their eyes. *(Deut. 30:1-5)* They cannot claim the Rabbis "changed" these verses, since they were truly fulfilled.

Therefore, the defensive wars Israel fought to defend Israel's right to our Allah-given land cannot constitute murder. If Israel wanted to do to the Palestinians as the Germans did to the Jews, they would have quite easily and systematically massacred the Palestinians long ago. On the contrary – even against the laws of war in the Torah – Israel's liberal defense establishment puts Jewish soldiers at risk, fighting surgical wars that even fail to eradicate the rogues at the helm of terrorist organizations, who themselves are impious Moslems. Meanwhile, Israel supplies those wicked regimes with electricity and allows the flow of cash into their banks. Again, this is not for lack of the power to crush such criminals, but out of misplaced compassion for those who are not only out for Jewish and American blood, but brutally oppress their own.

Allah's enduring love for the Jews is according to another principle that Allah does not change His mind precariously, as prophet Malachi (another true prophet in Moslem eyes) wrote, *"I, HaShem, do not change" (Malachi 3:6).* Prophet "Daoud" (King David) confirmed Allah's eternal love for Israel in his prayer, *"And You established for Yourself Your people Israel to be Your people ["a people unto You"] forever, and You, HaShem, became their God." (II Samuel 7:24)*

When will more Moslems open their eyes, and recognize Allah's enduring love and Providence for Israel? When will they note how – while the indeed Jews fell from the observance of Allah's laws, bringing upon them much suffering and degradation – the nation has been steadily returning to the strict observance of Allah's laws for Israel?

Those laws – *even the teachings of the Rabbis* – are explicitly referred to in the Qur'an as having been given to the Jews by Allah:

> "We [*Allah*] have revealed the [Written and Oral] *Torah*, in which there is guidance and light. By it the prophets who surrendered themselves judged the Jews, and so did the rabbis and the *Torah* scholars, according to God's Book which had been committed to their keeping and to which they themselves were witnesses."
> [*Qur'an, The Table, Sura 5:44*]

And according to *Nebi Musa* ("prophet Moses") those laws are eternal, never to be replaced, as it is written: "an eternal law for all your generations." *(Lev. 3:17 and another 7 places)* I would then conclude with the fact that, according to Israel's eternal Torah from Allah, *Allah Commanded that Israel bring all of mankind to the Seven Laws of Noah.* There should be *nothing* in the Seven Laws that any intelligent, sincere Moslem should find offensive, if he would only approach the subject honestly and objectively, with no hate in his heart.

15) **Increasingly, Jews and the Jewish state are being portrayed as the chief cause of global terrorism, and the source of my country's woes. While I know this is a result of increasing influence of the left wing-Muslim alliance in the press, I myself feel angry when Jewish arch-criminals are exposed, and when the Jewish state acts against its own people. Being that many ultra-Orthodox oppose the state for not representing Torah values, I too, at times, feel inclined to criticize Israel. As a God-fearing Noahide and a citizen of my own country, where should my loyalties lie? Moreover, how do I answer those who criticize the Jews and Israel?**

Loyalty to the Honor of HaShem

The Noahide's first loyalty should be to the honor of God's Name. Standing by the cause of the Jews and Israel is not a statement that the Jews are the most righteous people on earth at this time. Rather, it is a statement of loyalty to *HaShem's* honor. From over 2,500 years, prophet Ezekiel foresaw how Israel would be gathered back to its land from all the countries of its dispersion not for their own sake (not for the sake of their righteousness), but for the honor of His Name:

Therefore say unto the house of Israel: Thus says *HaShem* God: *I do not this for your sake, O house of Israel, but for My holy name, which you have profaned among the nations to where you came.* And I will sanctify My great Name, which has been profaned among the nations, which you have profaned in the midst of them; and the nations shall know that I am *HaShem,* says *HaShem* God, when I shall be sanctified through you before their eyes. *For I will take you from among the nations, and gather you out of all the countries, and will bring you into your own land.*

For the return and renewed vitality of the Jewish People in the land of their ancestral heritage after 2,000 years – a phenomenon that defies natural explanation – is the greatest testimony to His Kingship of the world.

Loyalty to Truth and Fairness

Secondly, a Noahide's loyalty should be to truth and fairness. Whatever makes negative press about Jews and Israel, due to Israel's increasing political isolation, makes big news. However, such press – even when factual – cannot be imagined to represent the noble, multi-faceted, optimistic, creative, brilliant, Israeli masses, particularly not the growing Torah community. And the Noahide must understand that despite threat of expulsions, the welfare and security of Torah Jewry in Israel are still inexorably tied to that of the secular state. For a Torah-based refutation of the claims of religious anti-Zionists, see Appendix III.

That being said, the day when non-Jewish friends of Israel boldly take to the streets *en masse* in cities around the world to loudly protest the expulsion of Jews from their homes – just as they do today to protest Israel's surgical wars against its mortal enemies – is the day we might begin to see an end to the madness.

The Growing Illusion of a Conflict of Loyalties

In response to those who feed the growing illusion of a conflict of loyalty between Israel and one's country, a Noahide is morally obligated to know and promote the truth. No matter how loud the voices demonizing the Jews and Israel, this will not change the significant and continual flow of blessing to the world from Jews in Israel and abroad – particularly the U.S. These are discussed in Part III.

Rather than allow oneself to be convinced by the growing tirade, God-fearing friends of the Jewish People must shrewdly expose the causes of this increasing trend, and raise their own voices to match the lies being spread.

Even in a country with as free a press as the U.S., the media has historically been one of the key organs of power utilized by any successful government. The intensifying demonization of Jews and Israel even in the American media cannot be separated from the growing policy of appeasement to Islam by the White House. While outreach to Islam began with President George W. Bush, it changed direction and intensified in February 2009, when the newly-elected President Obama dropped the phrase "war on terror" from its diplomatic lexicon. (3) In April 2010, the terms "Islam," "Jihad" (4) and even "Islamic radicalism" (5) were eliminated from diplomatic rhetoric as well. In both cases, positive pieces about each move were created by the Associated Press, openly describing the decisions as "courting the Muslim community" and "an outreach gesture to Islam" respectively.

This cannot be unrelated to another move by the Obama administration *in the same month* as the latter change in official White House rhetoric: to cancel increased security restrictions placed by American security officials on travelers from Cuba and 13 Muslim countries – known exporters of terror including Afghanistan, Iraq, Iran, Lebanon, Libya, Somalia, Sudan, Syria, and Yemen. (6)

Whoever is convinced that the threats of Islamic terror and jihad have indeed proven to be misnomers that no longer should be used, dangers that no longer need be heeded, should also be convinced that an important ally of the U.S. as Israel has now become the source of her ills.

Preparing For The Future

16) What is the best way to help the Noahide movement to grow?

There are a number of models and examples that suggest that, while outreach is a high priority, the best and surest way for a devout religious movement to grow is by *reproduction*. Consider the tremendous rise of the influence of Islam in only the last few decades, simply due to their alarming increase in numbers. Save a dramatic act of Divine intervention, Westerners cannot hope to counter that influence – not in short or long term – without re-learning the art of raising large families, staying together, and serious community building.

One of the reasons for this is, despite the great importance of outreach, authentic teachings (loyal to the true Oral tradition) tend to become diluted through mass outreach, due to the need to make Torah more palatable to the wide public and easier for the masses to adopt. Moreover, only a minority of converts remain sincere over the long term. *Therefore the surest way for Noahides to build a better world is to create a better generation — raising as many pure, properly-educated children as they can responsibly afford.*

I therefore suggest that Noahides adopt a program like the Mormon Church, which gives the task of conducting vigorous outreach to the young, who go on missions before getting married. Afterwards, *single adults should focus primarily on getting married,* and married couples must invest their best efforts in building large, quality families and planning strong, sheltered communities. In the long term, only closed, tight-knit Noahide communities can provide the strong mutual support necessary for growing Noahide families, and provide quality education and a healthy social atmosphere in which children can grow up, sufficiently insulated from the awful trappings of mainstream culture.

This is the Israelite model followed by devout Hebrews from the house of Jacob down to the "ultra-Orthodox" in the modern state of Israel. As one can see purely based on demographic trends in Israel over the last 62 years, it has been – with *HaShem*'s blessing – greatly effective.

17) **It seems clear that the time of the Final Redemption is nearer than ever. The Bible spells out in no uncertain terms the Divine retribution that the nations of the world will suffer, outside of the Land. How is a non-Jew to prepare and protect himself from God's Wrath in these turbulent times?**

As noted previously, *HaShem* promised Abraham, *"And I will bless them that bless thee, and I will curse him that curses you..." (Genesis 12:3)* Those who fulfill the Seven Laws with an unshakeable faith in the God of Israel and His plan for mankind, and express an unwavering support for the Jewish People and their full sovereignty over the Land of Israel, can hope to see this blessing.

However, as we learn from the patriarch Jacob in his preparations for his much-feared encounter with his brother Esau *(Genesis ch.32,33), faith and Torah observance alone do not obviate even a righteous man from the need to invest his best efforts to enhance his chances of survival in the tumultuous times that lie ahead.* I side with those conservative voices who encourage people everywhere to (a) invest their assets in real gold, not merely gold bonds, (b) learn natural ways to store food, (c) learn natural medicine and other survival skills, (d) practice living "off the grid" (without electricity or telephones) and (e) learn an effective non-idolatrous martial art, such as 52 Hand Blocks. That is, until *Qesheth* Hebrew Warrior Arts becomes widely available to Noahides. However, for a number of reasons, I do *not* recommend that Noahides attempt to acquire firearms, even legally.

Day-To-Day Practical *Halakhah*

18) What meat sold today can a Noahide consume?

As we learned in Part II, Noahide Law #6, meat that is kosher for Noahide consumption must have been removed from an animal only after it has completely ceased to convulse after slaughter or death by other means. If meat was removed before then, it is *ever min ha-hhai* – a "limb from the living." To knowingly eat such meat is a capital crime for non-Jews.

For example, one popular meat entree in the South and Central United States, is pure *ever min ha-hhai*: Battered and fried bull testicles (popularly known as "rocky mountain oysters"), removed from the poor creatures while they remain alive.

While this applies all species of mammals (including non-kosher species, such as pig), it does not apply to bird meat or fish. Therefore, *any* packaged fowl meat found in the market – be it chicken, turkey, goose, etc. – is kosher for Noahides, even in a Third World country where U.S. Food and Drug Administration standards do not exist! However, meat from any mammal must be cut up according to Noahide law, for it to be kosher for non-Jews.

Since the passage of the Humane Slaughter Act (HMSLA) in 1958, and the subsequent Farm Bill (Public Law 107-171) signed into law in May 2002, ensuring that the HMSLA be fully enforced, *we understand that USDA-approved meat can be relied on by Noahides.* (7) We questioned this at first, when we learned that federal law only requires that the animal be rendered unconscious (not actually dead), and that not all methods are 100% effective. However, we have learned that before actual cuts of meat headed for butcheries are removed from the body, the creature's blood is drained, and the body is halved and quartered. By the time cuts of meat for consumption are removed, there is virtually no chance the animal's parts are still convulsing or cardiovascular system still working. The creature is fully dead.

Nevertheless, there is a slight possibility that, since the hooves are cut off early on in the process, it is possible that they were removed before the convulsions fully ceased. While this may not be widespread enough to make hoof meat forbidden, a God-fearing Noahide should refrain from these cuts with nothing more than USDA-approval.

One way a Noahide can have greater certainty that his meat comes from a slaughterhouse that was particularly strict in its treatment of animals, is only buying meat certified with the label "Certified Humane Raised and Handled." This requires an even higher standard for slaughtering farm animals than HMSLA: the American Meat Institute Standards (AMI). More information can be found at Humane Farm Animal Care website, *www.certifiedhumane.org*.

The inhumane ways that livestock are generally raised and slaughtered, even in modern "kosher" slaughterhouses, affects the quality of the meat. Moreover, meat from livestock not left to graze is lacking in nutrition. For these reasons and more, my family will not consume any meat *except the meat of livestock left to graze* that was acquired and slaughtered by an exceptional private butcher we know. Although it is not required, it is my non-*halakhic* suggestion to Noahides that they aspire to this ideal as well.

19) What book should a Noahide pray from? From the Jewish siddur (traditional prayer book), or is there a prayer book for Noahides? If there there are more than one, how can I know which one is best?

Being that Noahide prayer is purely voluntary, so long as one prays directly to the Creator with proper belief and intent, there are no rules or guidelines to Noahide prayer. He need not pray from a book at all, but pray to *HaShem* in his own words, be they written down, or spontaneous. He may do so out loud, quietly, or in silent meditation. He may do so in any position: standing, sitting, or even while lying down on his bed.

The value of personal prayer is much underrated in our times. Fortunately, thanks to the widespread appeal of the teachings of Rebbe Nahman of Breslov in this generation, the truth taught in Bible and *Mishneh Torah* – that *HaShem* listens to the simple, heartfelt words from the hearts of ordinary people – is beginning to re-enter mainstream Jewish thought. *(See Book of Love, Laws of Prayer and Priestly Blessing 5:14[13], Laws of Blessings 10:28[26], etc.)*

If the Noahide wishes to pray from a book, he may choose to recite the psalms of King David, or pray from a formal *siddur* – be it a Noahide prayer book or Jewish *siddur*. He may even imitate Jewish prayer in all its details.

The only trap Noahides must avoid is creating new religious rites – ceremonies or customs of worship that are regarded as obligatory. As explained in Part II, Section B-1h: While a community or an individual may choose their own prayer structure or develop their own, they may not to relate to it as cast in stone. In short, since the *halakhah* has left the world of prayer open as a matter of personal choice for Noahides, it should remain that way.

That being said, there is wisdom in walking in the footsteps of Torah scholars. There is only one Noahide prayer book prepared by rabbis that I am aware of: *Service from the Heart*, produced by the Oklahoma B'nei Noah Society, with approbations from Rabbis Yoel Schwartz and Yechiel Sitzman in Jerusalem. We look forward to the prayer book being developed by Noahide scholar and teacher Adam Penrod and Rabbi Chaim Richman, which is partly based on the *siddur* of Rav Sa`adiah Gaon.

20) **Where should I prioritize my charity money? Should I give locally, to a disaster relief fund, or to a Jewish institution in Israel?**

Again, since charity is purely voluntary for Noahides, it is a personal decision. The model of Israelite *halakhah* is that one should prioritize a poor family member before anyone else, the poor of one's extended household before the poor of one's city, and the poor of one's own city over the poor of another city. This is according to the order hinted at in the verse *(Deut. 15:12)*: "...you shall surely open your hand to your brother, to your poor, and your needy in your land." *(Book of Seeds, Laws of Gifts to the Poor 7:13[12])*

However, Noahides are in no way limited by this value. They may prefer to prioritize or even give exclusively to their struggling Noahide brothers and sisters, or Torah scholars in Israel struggling to feed their families, over their own family. It is entirely a matter of personal discretion."

21) *I want to fulfill more Torah Commandments, yet I do not want to mislead others that I am a Jew. Can I – as a Noahide – fulfill Commandments such as mezuzah, tzitzith and tefillin? If so, how?*

The answer to this question is fully treated in Part II Section B-4a. In general, although a Noahide may certainly perform these Commandments (as non-obligatory good deeds) and receive eternal reward, he should do so in such a way that he will not be mistaken for a Jew, and be seen doing something that is forbidden to observant Jews – such as eating a cheeseburger or driving on the Sabbath day.

NOTES

(1) This and other sources in this response were found in: Kaplan, Aryeh, "Behold the Man: The Real Jesus" in *A Jewish Response to Missionaries*, published by National Conference of Synagogue Youth/Orthodox Union, New York NY 1997 (fifth printing). 106 pp.

(2) Translated passages from the *Qur`an* are from the teachings of Sheikh Abdul Hadi Palazzi, disseminated by Root & Branch Association, Ltd.

(3) Baldor, Lolita C., *Obama Administration Drops 'War on Terror'*, February 2, 2009. an Associated Press web-article at: *www.washingtonexaminer.com/politics/War-on-terror-catchphrase-not-Obamas-style38796857.html*

(4) Associated Press staff, *Obama Bans Terms Jihad, Islam*, July 4, 2010. A web-article at:__*www.jpost.com/International/Article.aspx?id=172576*

(5) Miskin, Maayana, *New Focus: Obama to Remove "Islamic Radicalism" from Documents*, April 8, 2010. A web-article at: *israelnationalnews.com/News/News.aspx/136917*

(6) Ben Gedalyahu, Tzvi, 'Terror-prone' US Allies Force Obama to Relax Airport Security, April 4, 2010. A web-article at: *israelnationalnews.com/News/News.aspx/136834)*

(7) Entry for "Humane Slaughter Act" at *Wikipedia: The Free Encyclopedia*, found at: *en.wikipedia.org/wiki/Humane_Slaughter_Act*

APPENDIX I

Structure Of The 14 Books Of *Mishneh Torah* *

NOTE: The legal sections in which the sources cited in this book are found are in boldface.

THE BOOK OF KNOWLEDGE

"I include in it all the commandments that are the basic principles of the religion of Moshe [Moses] Our Teacher, which one needs to know at the outset — such as recognizing the unity of the Holy One blessed be He and the prohibition of idolatry."

- **Laws of the Foundations of the Torah**
- **Laws of Personal Dispositions**
- Laws of Torah Study
- **Laws of Idolatry and Gentile Customs**
- **Laws of Repentance**

THE BOOK OF LOVE

"I include in it the commandments that are done frequently, which we have been commanded to do so that we may always love God and remember Him constantly — such as reading the *Shema*`, prayer, *tefillin*, and blessings; circumcision is included, because it is a sign in our flesh to constantly remind us when we are not in *tefillin* or *tzitzit* or the like."

- Laws of Reading the *Shema*`
- **Laws of Prayer and Priestly Blessing**
- Laws of Tefillin, Mezuzah, and Torah Scroll
- **Laws of Tzitzit**
- Laws of Blessings
- **Laws of Circumcision**

THE BOOK OF TIMES

"I include in it the commandments to be done at fixed times — such as Sabbath and holidays."

- **Laws of the Sabbath**
- **Laws of `Eruvin**
- Laws of Rest on the Tenth of Tishri
- Laws of Rest on the Holidays
- Laws of Leaven and Unleavened Bread
- Laws of Shofar, Sukkah and Lolav
- Laws of Sheqels
- Laws of the Sanctification of Months
- Laws of Fasts
- Laws of the Scroll of Esther and Hanukkah

THE BOOK OF WOMEN

"I include in it the commandments on sexual relations — such as marriage and divorce, levirite marriage and release from it."

- **Laws of Marriage**
- Laws of Divorce
- Laws of Levirate Marriage and Release
- Laws of the Virgin Maiden
- Laws of a Woman Suspected of Adultery

THE BOOK OF HOLINESS

"I include in it the commandments on forbidden sexual relations and commandments on forbidden foods — for in these two matters the Omnipresent sanctified us and separated us from the nations, in forbidden sexual relations and forbidden foods, and of both it is written 'and I have set you apart from the peoples' *(Leviticus 20,26)*, 'who have set you apart from the peoples' *(Leviticus 20,24).*"

- **Laws of Forbidden Sexual Relations**
- Laws of Forbidden Foods

Appendix I

- **Laws of Slaughter**

THE BOOK OF PROMISING

"I include in it commandments by which one undertakes to forbid himself in certain things — such as oaths and vows."

- Laws of Oaths
- **Laws of Vows**
- Laws of the Nazirite
- Laws of Appraisals and Devoted Property

THE BOOK OF SEEDS

"I include in it commandments on seed of the land — such as Sabbatical years and Jubilees, tithes and heave offerings, and the other commandments akin to these matters."

- **Laws of Diverse Varieties**
- **Laws of Gifts to the Poor**
- **Laws of Heave Offerings**
- Laws of Tithes
- Laws of Second Tithes and the Fruit of the Fourth Year
- Laws of First Fruits and Other Priestly Gifts Outside the
- Sanctuary
- Laws of the Sabbatical Year and the Jubilee

THE BOOK OF SERVICE

"I include in it commandments on building the sanctuary and continual public sacrifices."

- **Laws of the Chosen House**
- Laws of the Vessels of the Sanctuary and Those Who Serve in It
- **Laws of Entry into the Sanctuary**

- Laws of Things Forbidden on the Altar
- **Laws of Sacrificial Procedures**
- Laws of the Daily Offerings and Additional Offerings
- Laws of Sacrifices Become Unfit
- Laws of the Service on Yom Kippur
- aws of Benefit from Consecrated Things

THE BOOK OF SACRIFICES

"I include in it commandments on sacrifices of the individual."

- Laws of the Pesach Sacrifice
- Laws of Pilgrimage Festival Sacrifices
- Laws of the First-Born
- Laws of Unintentional Sins
- Laws of Those with Incomplete Atonement
- Laws of Substitution for Consecrated Animals

THE BOOK OF RITUAL PURITY

"I include in it commandments on ritual purity or impurity."

- Laws of the Uncleanness from a Corpse
- Laws of the Red Heifer
- Laws of Uncleanness from Leprosy
- Laws of Uncleanness of a Bed or Seat
- Laws of Other Sources of Uncleanness
- Laws of Uncleanness of Foods
- Laws of Vessels
- Laws of Ritual Baths

THE BOOK OF INJURIES

"I include in it commandments on civil relations in which there is injury at the offset to either property or person."

Appendix I

- Laws of Injury to Property
- **Laws of Theft**
- Laws of Robbery and Lost Property
- Laws of One Who Injures Person or Property
- Laws of a Murderer and the Preservation of Life

THE BOOK OF ACQUISITION

"I include in it commandments on sale and purchase."

- Laws of Sales
- Laws of Acquisition of Ownerless Property and Gifts
- Laws of Neighbors
- Laws of Agents and Partners
- **Laws of Slaves**

THE BOOK OF JUDGMENTS

"I include in it commandments on other civil relations in cases that do not have at the outset any injury — such as deposits, debts, and claims and denials."

- **Laws of Hiring**
- Laws of Borrowed and Deposited Things
- Laws of Creditor and Debtor
- **Laws of Claimant and Respondent**
- Laws of Inheritances

THE BOOK OF JUDGES

"I include in it commandments that are delegated to the Sanhedrin — such as capital punishment, receiving evidence, and administration of the king and his wars."

- **Laws of the Sanhedrin and Penalties Under Their Jurisdiction**
- Laws of Evidence
- **Laws of Rebels**

- Laws of Mourning
- **Laws of Kings and Wars**

* Copied with permission from the *Mechon Mamre* website, http://www.mechon-mamre.org/e/e0003.htm, and restructured by the author.

APPENDIX II

Understanding the Oral Tradition of *Hashem's* Incomparable Oneness

The sublime statement of faith recited by Jews, morning and night is: "Hear O' Israel, *HaShem* is our God, *HaShem* is **One**." According to Oral tradition, that Oneness is not as simple as it may seem to those who have not given it much thought:

> This God is One. He is not merely 'not two or more', but One such that there is none like his oneness among the unities in the universe. Not "one" such as a single category that includes other single entities, and not "one" such as a body that is divisible into different parts and extremities; but rather a oneness such as there is none like it in the universe. *(M.T. Laws of Foundations of Torah 1:5[7])*

It is not coincidental that the Catholic church, who historically did more to extinguish the light of the Oral law than anyone else (putting the Talmud "on trial" by staging public debates between rabbis and priests, staging public burnings of the Talmud), is a religion that declares God to be a trinity, including a "Son", who walked the earth as a god-man.

Elohim: a Sacred Name with Singular Meaning when Referring to HaShem

The source most touted for God being a plurality is the very first verse of the Torah: *"In the beginning, **Elohim** created the* *heavens and the earth."* The sacred Name of God used in that sentence and so many that follow, has the ending *"-im"* – the plural masculine noun-ending in Hebrew. *What the priests and followers of UFO-cults too seldom consider, is how the Oral tradition on that Name, that it is a singular form, is firmly rooted in the Written Torah itself.*

The simple, unlearned masses accept the teachings of their clergy on faith. However, the Catholic priests of the Middle Ages – who studied the Bible in Hebrew – had little excuse. How did they feel when they encountered the names of individual men in the Torah whose names have that "plural" ending? Consider Ephra*im*, son of Jacob. He was a singular individual. Ephraim is no isolated example. Consider his cousins Mupp*im* and Hupp*im* – two of the ten sons of Benjamin. *(Gen. 46:21)* We know they were individuals and not twins because of how they are counted. They are mentioned as part of the Torah's tally of 70 souls who made up Jacob's household, which descended into Egypt *(46:8-27)*: *The singular meaning of the end form "-im" is not unique to that sacred Name of God; it is found among names of individuals in the Bible.*

The following verse is another example that illustrates the singular meaning of the Name:

> And *HaShem* said to Moses: *'See,* I have set you to be *elohim* to Pharaoh [meaning "in God's stead"]; and Aaron your brother shall be your prophet.' (Ex. 7:1)

If the Name *Elohim* were plural, how could Moses be that to Pharaoh? The Name of God is being used as *a title for a single individual,* so that Moses could fully understand the role he was to fulfill. The Name clearly has singular meaning.

In truth, one need not look further than that very first Torah verse: *"In the beginning, Elohim created..."* The Hebrew word

174

Appendix II

for "created" – *bara*, is in the singular form. The past plural form of the verb "created" is *bar'u*. *The singular verb form in the verse declares the Oneness of the subject, "Elohim."*

His Incomparable Oneness

The above sources will do little to convince die-hards who cling to a mystical belief that "the One is Three, and the Three are One." However, the Oral tradition claims the opposite. *HaShem's Oneness is utterly indivisible.* How can we know which doctrine is true for certain?

Interestingly enough – although this may sound confusing at first – the classical Christian concept of God is true about a live human being. As RaMBaM teaches, a physical being is actually three entities in one: (1) the physical person himself, (2) his soul or life force, and (3) his *da'ath* (his consciousness, awareness or knowledge). (While these are unified during one's life, they separate when they person loses consciousness, and when he dies.) *If HaShem's* Oneness were such a unity, we would worship three united entities: *HaShem, His Life, and His Awareness or Knowledge. Yet HaShem is perfectly one in every aspect: something that our finite minds cannot grasp.* (M.T. Laws of Foundations of Torah 2:13[10])

Whoever claims this is purely rabbinical philosophy or an Oral tradition that is un-rooted in Scripture, should consider Isaiah 40:25: *"To whom will you liken Me, that I can be compared?"* If *HaShem* were a trinity, he could be compared to a living being. Moreover, if He would descend to earth adopting a physical form, he could be compared to an angel – as the angel who appeared to the parents of Samson in a physical form, only to leap into fire and ascend to Heaven, to the non-physical realm. *(Judges ch.1319-20)* Similarly, in the prophetic song Moses taught the Israelites, they sang: *"Who is like you among the mighty powers, HaShem?" (Ex. 15:11) HaShem* is beyond any comparison to the angels, to the stars, or to the mighty forces of nature such as rain – which descends to earth.

If *HaShem* were to descend to earth in a physical form and live a human life, then that aspect of Him would undergo change. What, then, do we do with the principle taught in Malachi 3:6: *"I, HaShem, do not change...?"* And if, as some Christians claim, He did so in order that He would fully know our suffering, can any believing person rightly imagine there is anything outside of *HaShem*'s full understanding? Could "the Judge of all the earth" *(Gen. 18:25)* not fully understand those whom He Judges? Could it be that the "Wise King" *(Proverbs 20:26)* does not understand His subjects; the One who "searches out the compartments of the heart" *(Proverbs 20:27)* – the God who "sees the heart", while man can only see the outward appearance?! *(I Samuel 16:7)*

With that principle in mind that *HaShem* does not change, and therefore does not physically descend to earth, note the places in the Bible where He is mentioned as "dwelling" in different places. He is mentioned in no uncertain terms as "sitting" or "dwelling" on earth – upon the cherubim (the angelic figures that adorned the cover of the Ark). *(I Samuel 4:4, II Samuel 6:2, II Kings 19:15)*. Yet He is referred in Psalms 2:4 as "sitting" or "dwelling" in Heaven. It should be clear by now that He "dwells" not by means of a body. Rather this refers to *HaShem* who causes His Presence to be sensed in the Heavens, and felt on earth. *HaShem – who does not change – neither has nor needs a physical form to do this.*

This also negates the popular, false notion that "God is everywhere, and in all things." I treated this and other false ideas in my commentary to the Noahide prohibition of Idolatry *(Part II, Section A)*. However, consider how the Bible itself negates this concept in the narrative of the prophet Elijah's experience on Mt. Sinai:

Appendix II

> And He said: 'Go forth, and stand upon the mount before *HaShem*.' And, behold, *HaShem* passed by, and a great and strong wind rent the mountains, and broke apart the rocks before *HaShem*; *but HaShem was not in the wind*; and after the wind an earthquake; *but HaShem was not in the earthquake*; and after the earthquake a fire; *but HaShem was not in the fire*; and after the fire a still small voice. *(I Kings 19:11-12)*

Although He May cause His Presence to be felt and manifested through nature; *HaShem* Himself is clearly separate from it. *What fills all creation is His limitless power and might. (M.T.* Book of Love, Laws of Blessings *10:16[14])*

The nature of God's Oneness and the truth of the Name *Elohim* are but one example of a number of apparent contradictions in Scripture that can only be fully resolved by an outside explanation by an accompanying tradition.

I hope the reader can begin to see the relationship between the Written Law and the Oral tradition. While the Written Law treats this deep subject with terse, subtle statements scattered across the Bible *(and that, amidst dozens of anthropomorphisms (verses that speak of HaShem in human terms by way of metaphor), the Oral tradition is her natural voice of explanation – so that the truth of the matter would never be lost.*

APPENDIX III

Refuting the Arguments of Anti-Zionist Torah Scholars

The premature, failed attempt by warriors of Ephraim to conquer the Land of Israel *(I Chronicles 7:20-22 cf. Midrash Rabbah Shir haShirim 2:7)* is one of the sources commonly cited in the Torah position against modern Zionism. By using this source in my discussion on children's education, *there was no intent to infer my agreement with the spurious arguments of the anti-Zionists, HaShem-forbid.*

This book is not the venue for a full, proper presentation of the case of authentic Torah Zionism — the belief that Jews are obligated to take initiative in returning to the land of Israel and establishing a Jewish commonwealth according to Torah Law, without waiting for the advent of the Messiah-king. In the realm of Torah scholarship, the work has already been done: A full refutation of these arguments is found in the seminal work of Rabbi Shlomo Teichtal, *Eim haBanim Semeichah*, available in English through Urim Publications. *(www.urimpublications.com)*

Nevertheless, I will present a few counter-arguments against the forces of darkness that persist within the Torah community, in hopes of "inoculating" Noahides against their misguided teachings.

Unlike the Egyptian and Babylonian exiles, the current Edomite exile never had a widely-known prophetic "end date". The oath that Israel allegedly swore to *HaShem* as they went into exile following the destruction of the Second

Temple *(Talmud, tractate Kethuboth 111a)* not to "go up like a wall" (conquer Israel by massive force) is in the realm of *midrash aggadah* (legend and homily), and has no legal import whatsoever. Consider the following:

- The oaths of *Kethuboth 111a* are not so much as mentioned in *Mishneh Torah*, the encyclopedic Code of Jewish Law. They could not possibly have legal import, since Jewish law is not decided on the basis of *midrash aggadah* (legend and homily). Moreover, *it remains an active rabbinical injunction that Jews must dwell in the Land.* (Laws of Kings & Wars 5:15[12])

  There is nothing in the law limiting how many Jews may return home to the land at any one time, or to what extent they are permitted to arm and defend themselves to ensure their survival. *Such quotas and limitations were imposed on the Jews by non-Jewish powers with anti-Semitic agendas; not by HaShem, and not by our Sages of blessed memory.*

- The above oath was mentioned in Talmud in the context of three other oaths, including two that the nations allegedly swore to *HaShem*: not to persecute the Jews too much and not to exterminate them. After the blood libels, crusades, Inquisition (in Europe and the Americas), the pogroms in Europe, the massacres of Jewish towns by Mohammed, and the holocausts; *the oaths of the nations have been violated — making the entire parcel invalid.*

  Even so, the oath that Israel not rebel against the nations of the world was not violated with the formation of the state of Israel, which was founded with the official agreement of the United Nations – the body representing the nations of the world.

Appendix III

- According to practical Torah law, the commandments associated with messianic times – anointing a king *(Laws of Kings 1:1-3[1-2])*, establishing the Great Sanhedrin and smaller high courts with a loyal police force in every city of Israel *(Laws of Sanhedrin 1:1-3[1-2])* and building the Temple *(Book of Service, Laws of the Chosen House 1:1)* – are Torah obligations on every generation of Jews, and do not depend on the advent of the Messiah-king.* This is full proof that Jews are always expected — whenever it becomes possible — to establish a Jewish state in the land of Israel when there is none, even by force.

But what can legitimize the shamefully secular, anti-Torah government that arose? It only arose out of the utter failure of the Torah-observant masses to immigrate to the Land, and participate in the formation of the government. However, *the need of the hour, a dire time of 'piquahh nefesh' — danger to Jewish life — would not wait for them or anyone.* It was the aftermath of the holocaust. Jews were being massacred by Arabs with the tacit approval of the wicked British colonial government (e.g., the Hebron massacre). At the same time, ships bringing starving Jewish survivors from Europe were being turned back off the very coast of Palestine... Whoever was present to erect a Jewish state did so out of fear for the very survival of the Jewish People. *Such conditions override nearly all Torah commandments. (Book of Seasons, Laws of the Sabbath 2:1)*

This does *not* excuse the wretched sins of the Israeli government, created by its apostate cronies over the years. However, it *does* show that the great miracles and biblical prophecies that were fulfilled *through* the state and its victories, and the mass return to Torah Judaism it unintentionally facilitated (in one of history's greatest ironies) were not an anomaly. All this has been through *HaShem*'s compassion and patience with His People, who are largely doing what they can, according to what they know, and under the most trying circumstances — *61 years of non-stop war, full control by a small Hellenistic elite, and deep societal divisions.*

---

* Although we do not learn definitive *halakhah* from RaMBaM's Commentary to the *Mishnah* (which he wrote in his youth) but rather from *Mishneh Torah*, there are instances in which RaMBaM's position in the latter work is understood more clearly by reviewing what he wrote in the former. In his Commentary to the *Mishnah*, discussing the first *mishnah* of tractate Sanhedrin, RaMBaM writes in clear and uncertain terms:

> *And I am of the opinion that the Sanhedrin will return before revelation of the Messiah, and it will be one his signs [of his legitimacy] — as it is said, "and I shall restore your judges as at first and your counselors as in the beginning, and afterwards your will be called 'the City of Righteousness.'" (Isaiah 1:26)*

In *Mishneh Torah*, even though a king must ideally be appointed by both prophet and Sanhedrin *(Laws of Kings and Wars 1:4[3])*, RaMBaM discusses the possibility of a conflict arising over who, between two individuals, should be anointed king. *(Ibid. 1:14[11-12]), Laws of Vessels of the Sanctuary 1:10[11])* In his Commentary to the *Mishnah (Kerethoth, Mishnah 1)*, we learn that such a controversy can be settled by a Sanhedrin (if it exists), a prophet (if there is a true prophet), the *Kohen-Gadol* (High Priest — if there is already a Temple), or even by the majority of the people of the nation, when they they choose to follow one over the other (in the case of there being no Sanhedrin, prophecy, or functioning *Kohen-Gadol*). In any case, the appointed king is anointed with *shemen ha-mish'hhah* — special anointing oil — in order to remove all doubt.

Appendix III

Elsewhere in *Mishneh Torah*, RaMBaM is very clear about the possibility that the king we anoint may not turn out to be the prophesied Messiah-king. *(Laws of Kings and Wars 11:6-9[3-4])*

The clear lesson here is that anointing a king, building a Temple, and restoring the Sanhedrin are serious national obligations that are not to be postponed. None of these obligations depend on the miraculous advent of the prophesied Messiah-king — only on the will of the nation.

(A special thanks to my friend, Rabbi David Bar-Hayim of Machon Shilo for his help on this subject.)

ABOUT THE AUTHOR

Mori Michael-Shelomo Bar-Ron is an ordained rabbi and publishing Torah scholar. He also has a BA in Anthropology from the University of California San Diego. His broad Torah journey ultimately brought him to formal rabbinical training at Shehebar Sephardic Center in Jerusalem, and under the tutelage of master halakhic decisors according to RaMBaM. During his period of involvement in an initiative by rabbis to restore the Sanhedrin, Mori Michael-Shelomo made strong bonds of friendship with Noahide scholars and teachers in the U.S., and became keenly aware of their need for authentic Torah instruction. *This was the inspiration for this book.*

He is currently based out of his Torah center in Ramat Beit Shemesh, *Ohel Moshe* (torathmoshe.com), where he continues to study, teach and write. A father of five children, Mori Michael-Shelomo makes a living as an English instructor. He is also an official spokesperson for, as well as an active, Wingate College-certified instructor-in-training of Abir/Qesheth Hebrew Warrior Arts – the ancient, traditional warrior art of the Jewish People.

* Mori Michael-Shelomo (pronounced *"Mee-kha-el She-lo-mo"*) prefers the title *m'ori* (מאורי), the humble title of the teachers of children in Yemen, over the title "rabbi."

www.ingramcontent.com/pod-product-compliance
Lightning Source LLC
Chambersburg PA
CBHW050146170426
43197CB00011B/1988